THE
SEARCH
FOR
SIGNIFICANCE
WORKBOOK

BUILD YOUR SELF-WORTH
ON GOD'S TRUTH

ROBERT S. MCGEE

LifeWay Press®
Nashville, Tennessee

ISBN 978-0-6331-9756-8 • Item 001244374

Dewey decimal classification: 155.2
Subject headings: VALUE \ SELF-ESTEEM \ CHRISTIAN LIFE

To order additional copies of this resource, write to LifeWay Resources Customer Service;
One LifeWay Plaza; Nashville, TN 37234; fax 615-251-5933; phone toll free 800-458-2772;
order online at LifeWay.com; or email orderentry@lifeway.com.

Printed in the United States of America

Groups Ministry Publishing • LifeWay Resources
One LifeWay Plaza • Nashville, TN 37234

CONTENTS

Looking Ahead

A FAMILY SQUABBLE

Case in point

Margie had called her mother to wish her a happy birthday. What started to be a pleasant conversation, however, suddenly turned sour. Instead of sounding happy that Margie called, she began to scold Margie for not visiting her often enough. Then when Margie related that her five-year-old son, Kevin, had a cough, Mom criticized Margie for not taking the child to the doctor sooner. She told Margie that if only she would insist that Kevin wear a sweater more often, he wouldn't get sick.

As tension mounted between mother and daughter, Margie quickly ended the conversation and hung up, absolutely furious at her mother for this turn of events. Then Margie felt guilty about being angry at Mom. After all, it was Mom's birthday.

Have you ever known anyone in Margie's situation, or have you found yourself in a similar circumstance? One in which you felt as angry and discouraged as she did and blamed yourself?

All of us have times when unpleasant life circumstances come along and knock the props out from under us, and we feel a sense of failure, rejection, guilt, shame, or all those emotions combined. These unpleasant circumstances can result from an everyday conversation between family members, such as in Margie's case. Margie received harsh criticism from another person. Any number of other situations can leave us feeling rejection, such as:

- Loss of a job
- Loneliness
- Feeling too busy
- Feeling misunderstood
- Death of a spouse or other loved one
- Imprisonment
- Failure to achieve a goal
- Physical or emotional abuse
- Experiencing hurt easily
- Experiencing frequent anger
- Living in poverty

If you can relate to any of these situations, and if you can relate to any of the negative feelings that stem from them, then *The Search for Significance Workbook* is for you. It is designed to help you change your thinking about the circumstances you encounter. It will reveal God as the source of your self-worth.

Course goal

After you complete a study of this workbook, you will be able to base your self-worth on the love, acceptance, and forgiveness of Jesus Christ and not on the world's standards, such as the approval of others or the ability to succeed at certain tasks.

To help you accomplish this goal, *The Search for Significance Workbook* will help you learn these things:

What's in it for you?

- **Four false beliefs** about yourself that result in painful emotions affecting your self-worth (p. 128).
- **The painful emotions,** or consequences, resulting from the four false beliefs. We allow these beliefs and their related emotions to control our behavior in life situations.
- **Truths from God's Word,** the Bible, that help you reject the false beliefs. We may not be able to change the situations we encounter, for these situations will occur in our lives day after day. What we can change is what we think or believe about those situations. When we change our focus, our emotions change as well. When our emotions change, our behavior also can change (p. 128).
- **The Holy Spirit's renewing of your mind** to replace those false beliefs and the harmful emotional responses that often result.
- **Memorization of God's Word** so you can hide God's truth in your heart and make it a part of your everyday life.
- **An affirmation,** or positive statement, based on God's truths. You can memorize "My Identity in Christ" (p. 113) and use it to reject the false beliefs as they arise.
- **How to take a Trip In,** a process in which you get in touch with what you really feel about a situation at times when you sense that your emotions could lead to destructive behavior. By identifying the emotion you feel, you learn to reject the false belief and then replace it with God's truth. See page 112.

On page 128 you will find the course map. On it you will find four false beliefs and God's truth. The affirmation "My Identity in Christ" is on page 113. Turn to these pages now (pp. 113, 128) and start to memorize them. By the end of the seven weeks of study, they will become a part of your everyday thoughts and vocabulary.

Who can benefit?

Everyone struggles to some degree with issues of self worth. Anyone can benefit from this study. They can use its helps in day-to-day dealings with people. People who have gone through failure or rejection can benefit from the course to help them develop a healthy identity based on Christ's unconditional love and acceptance. Likewise, people suffering from underlying emotional pain will benefit from the material's efforts to help them understand their pain. *The Search for Significance Workbook* offers a practical tool for dealing with issues of self worth.

The principles behind this study represent a lifelong learning process; therefore, individuals and groups may benefit from studying the course more than one time. The first time helps the reader to use these principles in thinking and conduct. Subsequent times help participants apply these principles to their lives over and over again until they master the process.

Study tips. Five days a week (which compose a unit, or week) you will be expected to study a segment of content material. You may need from 20 to 30 minutes of study time each day. Even if you find that you can study the material in less time, spread out the study over five days. This will give you more time to apply the truth to your life. Study at your own pace.

What will you do?

To achieve the full benefit of the educational design of *The Search for Significance Workbook*, prepare your personal assignments and participate in the group sessions. Study as if Robert S. McGee is sitting at your side helping you learn. When he asks you a question or gives you an assignment, respond immediately. Each assignment is indented and appears in **boldface type.** For example, an assignment will look like this:

> **Read Psalm 139:13. Write what the verse tells about God's care for you.**_____

In this activity, a line appears. You would write your answer on this line. Then, when you are asked to respond in a nonwriting manner—for example, by thinking about or praying about a matter—the type of assignment will give you a response line. Here is an example.

> **Think about an individual to whom you turn when you need encouragement. Stop and thank God for this person's role in your life.**

Activities are designed to help you learn the material more effectively. Do not deny yourself valuable learning by just glancing over the learning activities. Please do not assume that a nonwriting activity can be skipped because you do not "have to" respond.

In most cases you will get feedback about your response—for example, a suggestion about what you might have written. Personal answers are for this workbook only and do not have to be shared with the group.

Keep a Bible handy for times when the material asks you to look up Scripture. Memorizing Scripture and other elements such as the false beliefs, God's truth, and the affirmation are important parts of your work. Set aside a portion of your study period for memory work, beginning with the verse to know for that week. Then memorize the false beliefs, God's truths, and "My Identity in Christ." Make notes of problems, questions, or concerns that arise as you study. You will discuss many of these during your discovery-group sessions. Write these matters in the margins of this textbook so you can find them easily.

Sessions. Once each week you should attend *The Search for Significance* group session to help you discuss the content you studied the previous week, practice your memory work, share insights you have gained, look for answers to problems you encounter, and apply what you've learned to real-life situations.

If you have started a study of this resource and you are not involved in a group study, try to enlist some friends or coworkers who will work through this course with you. This book includes leader helps on pp. 114–25.

A key decision to this study is to trust Jesus as your Savior. If you have not done so, we encourage you to make this decision. You will benefit more from this course if you have already committed your life to Christ. But if you're not ready to make that decision just now, be aware that the need for this decision will be an ongoing emphasis. The material gives you opportunity to look at your relationship with Christ and to determine your need to commit your life to Him. How to begin a relationship with Christ is explained on page 22.

Getting the most from the course

Week 1
The Search Begins

TROUBLED RELATIONSHIPS

Dave was a handsome, highly successful business-man. He had always been able to live life on his own terms. To Dave, being strong meant being in control. He had used his strength as a way of controlling his wife and children. As a result, he was emotionally distant from his family. On the surface, everything looked fine.

But now he wept like a child. Life had caught up with Dave. Gone were his wife, his children, and much of what he had worked so hard for. Reality had turned the light on in Dave's world. He finally realized that the worst part of his world was himself. Now he longed to establish emotional closeness to his family, but he didn't know where to start.

A key verse to memorize this week:

> Search me, O God, and know my heart;
>   test me and know my anxious thoughts.
> See if there is any offensive way in me,
>   and lead me in the way everlasting.
>   **Psalm 139:23-24, NIV**

Words to help you understand this week's lessons:

redemption (n.)—Christ's delivering us from the curse of sin and death through His blood shed for us on the cross. He freed us from the guilt and power of sin.
*(Example: Because of Christ's **redemption** I am a new creature of infinite worth.)*

unconditional (adj.)—with no strings attached; without limitation; absolute.
*(Example: This week we study about God's **unconditional** love.)*

The purpose of this study is to help you build your self worth on a biblical basis by helping you—
• understand your own search for significance;
• recognize and challenge Satan's lies;
• apply God's truth to day-to-day life.

Day 1
The First Step

In the introduction you were asked to read the four false beliefs that Satan seeks to firmly fix in every person's mind (p. 112). In this week's Scripture, we are reminded of our need to search our hearts and minds to fully know the thoughts and feelings that guide our actions.

These false beliefs shape our thinking so much that we tend to react to certain life situations based on them. Have you ever found yourself asking, *Why in the world did I do that?* or *How did I let that happen?* If so, you probably made these remarks as a reaction to an unpleasant situation based on a false belief.

On page 4 you read about an unpleasant situation for Margie, who felt anger because her mother criticized her. Now it's your turn to write about your own experience.

Try to remember an unpleasant situation you found yourself in recently. In the margin describe the situation briefly. What did you feel?

Good news! God can transform our thought patterns from this world (the false beliefs) to His truth about us in His Word.

In the introduction you also read that what you believe about a situation creates certain emotions. We have listed those painful emotions, or consequences, for you here.

❏ The fear of failure   ❏ Guilt
❏ The fear of rejection   ❏ Shame

In the boxes beside these painful emotions, check any of the emotions you may have experienced recently.

Search for Significance will help you allow God to transform your thinking from the pattern of the world (the false beliefs) to His

Do not be conformed to this world, but be transformed by the renewing of your mind, so that you may prove what the will of God is, that which is good and acceptable and perfect.
Romans 12:2

truth about you in His Word, the Bible. We react to life situations based on a set of beliefs. We may not be able to change life situations we encounter, but we can change what we think or believe about those situations and how we act. Memorizing Bible verses is one of the ways we learn to reject false beliefs about ourselves and claim God's truth.

> If you continue in My word, then you are truly disciples of Mine; and you will know the truth, and the truth will make you free.
>
> John 8:31-32

"My Identity in Christ," found on page 113, focuses on God's truth and rejects the false beliefs that often control our minds. Memorizing this statement will help you recall it when you need to remember how much God cares about you.

Turning on the Light

This false belief system distorts our understanding of who we truly are in Jesus Christ. These examples help us see a reality in many of our lives.

Carl, an ambitious **father,** neglects his son, who grows up to take the responsibility of running the company. Although Carl had said he was retired, he still shows up for work each day and meddles with every decision his son makes. The son assumes that his father doesn't trust him. *He's never trusted me. Maybe I'm just not trustworthy,* he concludes.

Peggy, a **stay-at-home mother** with three children, painfully wonders, *Why don't I feel fulfilled as a homemaker?* She had thought children would fill that gaping hole in her life. Instead, her children were looking for affirmation from her. Sometimes it seemed she had little to give.

James, a **pastor,** preaches powerfully about God's **unconditional** love. He feels he must succeed in his ministry, but he is withdrawn around his family. He never has understood how to apply his sermons to his life and relationships.

Check the most appropriate statement.

❑ 1. The truth of God's Word is firmly implanted in the people in these stories.
❑ 2. One or more false beliefs about themselves control the people in these stories.

Because we aren't aware of how wounded we actually are, we can't take steps toward healing and health. We lack objectivity (looking at ourselves as though we were another person) to see the reality of our pain, hurt, and anger. Why do some of us lack objectivity? Why are we afraid to turn on the lights and experience the truth? Human beings develop creative ways to block pain and gain significance.

In the next paragraph underline the ways we block pain.

We suppress painful emotions by driving ourselves to succeed; or we withdraw; say hurtful things to people who hurt us, and punish ourselves when we fail. Sometimes we think good Christians don't have problems or feelings like ours. We try to make clever statements so people will accept us; we help people so they will appreciate us; and we say and do countless other unfulfilling things.

A sense of need usually prompts us to look for another choice. We may have the courage to examine ourselves and desperately want to change, but we may remain unsure about how and where to start. We may not want to look honestly within ourselves for fear of what we'll find, or fear that if we discover what's wrong, nothing can help us. Perhaps we think our situation is normal. We may think that enduring loneliness, hurt, and anger represent a normal experience for all persons. The good news? It's not.

Stop now and pray. Ask the Holy Spirit to help you look objectively at your life and to lead you to a person who can help you in the weeks ahead. When God directs you to that someone, write his or her name in the blank below.

Day 2
God Wants Us to Be Real

Some of us have deep emotional and spiritual scars from the neglect, abuse, and manipulation that often accompany living in a **dysfunctional family** (see definition). Others of us were blessed with healthier families. However, all of us suffer from the effects of our own sinful nature, not to mention the sins of others. Whether our hurts are deep or mild, we act wisely when we are honest about them. Then, we can experience growth and victory.

Many of us mistakenly believe that God doesn't want us to be honest about our lives. We think He will be upset with us if we tell Him how we really feel (as though He doesn't know). But God

Sometimes we think good Christians don't have problems or feelings like ours.

dysfunctional family (n.)— *a family in which alcoholism, drug abuse, divorce, absent father or mother, excessive anger, verbal and/ or physical abuse exists.*

11

tells us through the Scriptures that He does not want us to be shallow in our relationship with Him and others. Read John 17:21-22 in the margin.

... that they may all be one; even as You, Father, are in Me and I in You, that they also may be in Us, so that the world may believe that You sent Me. The glory which You have given Me I have given to them that they may be one, just as We are one.

John 17:21-22

Ask for God's guidance in the following areas. Underline the ones you will find most challenging.

1. To help me be honest with myself
2. To help me think the way God thinks.
3. To help me deal with my feelings
4. To know and apply God's truth to my life
5. To find a person with whom I can share and who will pray for me

Experiencing God's love does not mean that all of our thoughts, emotions, and behaviors will be pleasant and pure. It means that we can be *real* as we feel pain and joy, love and anger, confidence and confusion.

Self-worth, often called self-esteem or personal significance, is a sense of self-respect and a feeling of satisfaction with who we are. True self-worth, unlike pride, is not based on our performance nor the opinions of others.

What is your opinion about yourself? Mark the following statements as T (true) or F (false).

_____ 1. I am glad I am who I am.
_____ 2. I often wish I were someone else.
_____ 3. I like my personality.
_____ 4. I have a healthy sense of self-worth.
_____ 5. I see changes which I need to make in my life.
_____ 6. I am eager to trust God for wisdom and the discipline to make these changes.

A healthy self-concept develops when we recognize our value and worth. It involves understanding that we, as unique human beings, have certain gifts and abilities unlike those anyone else has. Each of us can contribute to the world in a special way.

A person with a healthy self-concept will experience the pain of failure and defeat, but that failure won't destroy that person. A person with a positive sense of self-esteem can enjoy personal strengths and can accept the fact that he or she has weaknesses. This represents a wholesome love for oneself.

Read Ephesians 1:3-14 in your Bible. Check the statements that correctly describe what God already has done for you.

❏ 1. God has blessed you with every spiritual blessing.
❏ 2. God has punished you because of your failures.
❏ 3. God has declared you holy and blameless.
❏ 4. God has forgiven you.
❏ 5. God at times has condemned and rejected you.
❏ 6. God has sealed you with the Holy Spirit.

You may feel very happy and thankful; you may be overwhelmed with how much God loves you; or you may be thinking, *This can't be true. I don't feel any of these things at all.* That's OK. It's better to be honest and to feel pain than to deny your discomfort and to try to convince yourself that you are happy. Remember, your feelings are not the basis of truth. God's Word is our authority. What it says is true, whether we feel it or not. The more we understand God's Word and live by it, the more our feelings will reflect His character and love. Hopefully, in the previous exercise you did not check numbers 2 or 5.

Here are some statements that we have made thus far. Underline the ones that are true.

• We need help to see ourselves objectively.
• The Lord wants us to be honest with Him and ourselves.
• Failure will destroy a person who has a healthy self-concept.
• God has blessed us with every spiritual blessing.
• God has chosen you, declared you holy and blameless, adopted you, redeemed you, and forgiven you.

God wants all people to achieve a balance between striving for excellence and being content with themselves, but relatively few of us experience that balance. From the beginning of life, we find ourselves on the prowl, searching to satisfy some inner, unexplained yearning. This yearning causes us to seek people who will love us. We strive for success as we drive our minds and bodies harder and farther. We hope that because of our sweat and sacrifice, others will appreciate us more.

What are some ways you have tried to achieve personal significance? I've given you one of my own as an example.

Making money _____ _____

Just as He chose us in Him before the foundation of the world, that we would be holy and blameless before Him.

Ephesians 1:4

The more we understand God's Word and live by it, the more our feelings will reflect His character and love.

A man or a woman who lives only for the love of others' attention is never satisfied—at least not for long. Our desire to be loved and accepted is the symptom of a deeper need—the need that often determines our behavior and is the primary source of our emotional pain. Often unrecognized, this desire represents our need for self-worth.

Day 3

Discovering Our True Worth

Some say the goal of self-worth is simply feeling good about ourselves. A more biblical goal goes far beyond that limited perspective. we want an accurate view of ourselves, God, and others, based on the truth of God's Word.

The thief comes only to steal and kill and destroy; I came that they might have life, and have it abundantly.
John 10:10

John 10:10, which appears in the margin, reminds us how much God treasures His creation. It reminds us that Christ came to earth so that people might experience life "abundantly," or fully. However, experiencing the abundant life God intends for us does not mean that our lives will be problem-free.

On the contrary, life itself is a series of problems that often act as obstacles to our search for significance. The abundant life is the experience of God's love, forgiveness, and power in the midst of these problems. The Scriptures warn us that we experience a warfare that can weaken our faith, lower our self-esteem, and lead us into depression. In his letter to the Ephesians, Paul instructed us to put on the armor of God (Godlike qualities that make us spiritually strong) so that we can be equipped for this type of spiritual battle (see Ephesians 6:13-17).

I am _____
_____
_____
_____

However, it often seems that unsuspecting believers are the last to know that this battle is occurring and that Christ in the end has won the war. They are surprised and confused by difficulties. They think the Christian life is a playground, not a battlefield.

I'm here because ____
_____
_____
_____

As Christians, our fulfillment in this life depends not on how skillfully we avoid life's problems but on how skillfully we apply God's specific solutions to those problems.

People wrestle with the basic questions, Who am I? and, Why am I here? In the margin write your thoughts on the answer you would give to those questions.

14

A correct understanding of God's truth is the first step toward discovering our significance and worth.

> An accurate, biblical self-concept contains both strength and humility, both sorrow over sin and joy about forgiveness, a deep sense of our need for God's **grace,** and a deep sense of the reality of God's grace.

In the margin read 1 John 1:9 and, in your own words, make it personal. Rewrite it, using *I, my,* and *me.*

Millions of people spend a lifetime searching for love, acceptance, and success without understanding the need that causes the quest. What a waste to attempt to change behavior without truly understanding the cause of such behavior! We can learn that God gave us a hunger for self-worth and only He can satisfy it. Our value does not depend on our ability to earn people's acceptance. People change their minds. Instead, true self worth is God's love and acceptance, which are unchanging. He created us. He alone knows how to fulfill all of our needs.

Listed below are examples of typical approval-seeking actions. Check the ones you can identify in your behavior.

- ❏ I sometimes change my position on something or alter what I believe because someone shows signs that they disapprove of me.
- ❏ In order to avoid someone's displeased reaction, I sometimes don't say what I mean.
- ❏ I sometimes flatter people to make them like me.
- ❏ I sometimes feel depressed or anxious when someone disagrees with me.
- ❏ I sometimes apologize for myself—the excessive "I'm sorry" designed to have others forgive me and approve of me all the time.

When God created human beings, He gave them a sense of purpose. When people rebelled against God, they lost that focus. Since then people have tried to find purpose and meaning apart from God. But God has made us in such a way that He only can meet our needs. Money, fame, fine houses, sports cars, and success in a job are only counterfeits of the true worth we have in Christ. Though these promise to meet our need for fulfillment, the things they provide are short-lived. God and His purposes alone can give us a wise, lasting sense of significance.

> If we confess our sins, He is faithful and righteous to forgive us our sins and to cleanse us from all unrighteousness.
>
> 1 John 1:9

15

Look below at each pair of statements. Check the one in each pair that indicates a self-worth based on God's acceptance.

❏ 1. I am recognized as one of the best in my field.
❏ 2. I am recognized as a child of God.

❏ 1. My boss at work really appreciates me.
❏ 2. My Lord totally accepts me.

❏ 1. I am successful in most projects I start.
❏ 2. I am deeply loved by God.

❏ 1. Everyone at work has noticed the change in me.
❏ 2. I am completely forgiven by the Father.

Does the world's system of evaluating a person govern how you act?

Does the world's system of evaluating a person govern how you act? The world's system goes against God's system, no matter what our standard of performance or whose approval we seek. Realizing that your worth does not depend on meeting some condition will free you from the fears of failure and rejection and will give you joy, thankfulness, and a desire to honor the One who loves you so much.

Underline the truths from our study today.

• The abundant life is the experience of God's love, forgiveness, and power in the face of life's problems.
• God has made us in such a way that He is the only One who can meet our need for significance.
• An accurate, biblical self-concept contains both strength and humility, both sorrow over sin and joy about forgiveness, both a deep sense of our need for God's grace and a deep sense of the reality of God's grace.

Day 4

The Origin of the Search

When the woman saw that the tree was good for food, and that it was a delight to the eyes, and that the tree was desirable to make one wise, she took from its fruit and ate; and she gave also to her husband with her, and he ate. Then the eyes of both of them were opened, and they knew that they were naked; and they sewed fig leaves together and made themselves loin coverings.
Genesis 3:6-7

In the Scriptures God tells us what we need to know in order to discover our true worth. The Old Testament tells us of sin and the fall of human beings into sin. Read Genesis 3:6-7 in the margin.

To understand the lasting effects of this event, we need to examine the nature of human beings before sin caused them to lose their sense of security and significance. The first created persons lived in intimate fellowship with God. They were secure and free. In all of God's creation, no creature compared to them. Indeed, Adam and Eve, the first persons, were magnificent creations, complete and perfect in the image of God, designed to reign over all the earth (Genesis 1:26-28).

Their purpose was to reflect the glory of God. God wanted to demonstrate His holiness through humankind (Psalm 99:3-5), love and patience (1 Corinthians 13:4), forbearance (1 Corinthians 13:7), wisdom (James 3:13,17), comfort (2 Corinthians 1:3-4), forgiveness (Hebrews 10:17), faithfulness (Psalm 89:1,2,5,8), and grace (Psalm 111:4). Through intellect, free will, and emotions, humankind was to be the showcase for God's glorious character.

Read Genesis 1:25-31 in your Bible and answer the following questions.

1. How do these verses show that God thought highly

   of people? (v. 26) _____

2. What are the two responsibilities God gave to

   humankind? (v. 28) _____

3. What was His evaluation of creation after He created

   people? (v. 31) _____

Compare what you wrote with these statements.

1. The fact that God made us in His image shows how highly He regards us.
2. God created people to bear God's image and to exhibit His glory. He gave humans two responsibilities—dominion over the earth and procreation, filling the earth with people who also bore God's image.
3. Genesis 1:31 reveals that God's view of creation changed from "good" to "very good" after He created humans.

   Before the first persons did a single deed, God said they were very good; therefore, the basis of God's evaluation could not have been their performance. The first persons were acceptable because God said they were.

> **Through intellect, free will, and emotions, humankind was to be the showcase for God's glorious character.**

Satan Enters the Picture

God also created Satan in perfection, just as He did Adam and his wife Eve. At the time God created him, Satan's name was Lucifer, which means *morning star.* Lucifer was an angel of the highest rank, created to glorify God. He was clothed with beauty and power and was allowed to serve in the presence of God.

Sadly, Lucifer's pride caused him to rebel against God. He and a third of the angels were cast from heaven (Isaiah 14:12-15; Revelation 12:7-9). When he appeared to Adam and Eve in the garden, he did so in the form of a serpent, "more crafty than any beast of the field which the LORD God had made" (Genesis 3:1).

God gave humans authority over the earth, but if they, like Lucifer, rebelled against God, they would lose both their authority and perfection. They would become a slave to sin (Romans 6:17) and subject to God's wrath (Ephesians 5:6). Therefore, destroying human beings was Satan's way to reign on earth. He thought it also would overthrow God's glorious plan for humanity.

The deeds of the flesh are evident, which are: immorality, impurity, sensuality, idolatry, sorcery, enmities, strife, jealousy, outbursts of anger, disputes, dissensions, factions, envying, drunkenness, carousing, and things like these, of which I forewarn you, just as I have forewarned you, that those who practice such things will not inherit the kingdom of God.
Galatians 5:19-21

Read Galatians 5:19-21. List the sins that Satan has used to try to overthrow God's glorious plan for us.

_____

_____

_____

In this morning's newspaper stories or in last night's TV news programs what did you read or see that showed people falling to temptation? List specific events.

_____

_____

_____

To accomplish his goal of overthrowing God's plan, Satan tempted Eve, who fell for his deception. Eve ate of the tree of the knowledge of good and evil. She believed it would make her wise and like God. Then Adam chose to forsake the love and security of God and to sin also.

By sinning, Adam and Eve not only lost the glory God had intended for humankind but also forfeited their close relationship and fellowship with God. Their deliberate rebellion also aided Satan's purpose. It gave Satan power and authority on earth.

Read Matthew 25:46 in the margin. According to this verse, what is the final outcome of fallen humanity?

These will go away into eternal punishment, but the righteous into eternal life.
Matthew 25:46

_____

_____

Today we see effects of the fall in personal problems, sickness, loneliness, suicide, disputes between people, murder, rape, war, or natural disasters such as drought, famine, and earthquakes.

From that moment on after humanity fell, all history led to a single hill outside Jerusalem, where God appointed a Savior to pay the penalty for people's sin of rebellion. Though we justly deserve God's anger because of that deliberate rebellion (our attempts to find security and purpose apart from Him), His Son became our substitute, experienced the wrath our rebellion deserves, and paid the penalty for our sins. Christ's death represents the most overwhelming evidence of God's love for us. Because Christ paid for our sins, our relationship with God is restored. We can experience His nature and character, commune with Him, and reflect His love to all the world.

Day 5
Your Relationship with Christ

We cannot understand the truths of God's Word with human wisdom alone. God the Father has given us the Holy Spirit as a free gift when we accept Jesus Christ as our Lord and Savior.

Stop for a moment and think about your relationship with Jesus Christ. Ask yourself the question, *Have I given my life to Jesus as my Savior and my Lord?* Before you go any further in this search for significance, settle this question. Without the free gift of salvation that is found only in Jesus Christ, you do not possess the Holy Spirit. Without the Holy Spirit you do not possess spiritual understanding, and you never will be able to accept what God's Word says about you. Turn to page 22 and read "Beginning a Relationship with Christ." Then return to this page.

God has freely given us our worth.

Only Christ Never Fails

We do not have to succeed or please others to have a healthy sense of self worth. God has freely given us our worth. Failure and/or others' disapproval can't take it away! It would be nice for my parents (or whomever) to approve of me, but if they don't approve of me, God still loves and accepts me.

Do you see the difference? The have-to mentality is sheer slavery to performance and to the opinions of others, but we are secure and free in Christ. We don't have to have success or anyone else's approval. Of course, it would be nice to have success and approval, but the point is clear: Christ is the source of our security; Christ is the basis of our worth; Christ is the only One who promises and never fails.

We can choose two possible options to determine our self-worth:

The world's system:

Self-worth = Performance (what you do) + others' opinions (what others think or say about you).

God's system:

Self-worth = God's truth about you

The World's System Versus God's System

The following are the four false beliefs that Satan uses to undermine God's purposes. Many of us apply them daily in our relationships and circumstances. Estimate to what degree, from 0 to 100 percent, you live by each of these false standards.

_____% I must meet certain standards to feel good about myself.

_____% I must have the approval of certain others to feel good about myself. (Without their approval I cannot feel good about myself.)

_____% Those who fail (including me) are unworthy of love and deserve to be punished.

_____% I am what I am. I cannot change. I am hopeless. I am the sum total of all my successes and failures, and I'll never be significantly different.

When we first begin to examine and confront these lies, the percentages may seem high. This is normal. In time these percentages should go down. They represent the beginning of change. To the extent that you believe these lies, the world's system influences your life. Each belief stems from the concept that your self-worth = performance + others' opinions.

This book is dedicated to the process of understanding, applying, and experiencing the basic truths of God's Word. In its chapters we will examine the process of hope and healing. Instead of the four false beliefs that Satan's deception generates, we will discover God's gracious, effective, and permanent solution to our search for significance.

Review this week's lessons. Pray, asking God to identify one or more positive statement(s) that had an impact on your understanding of who you are. Write this statement in your own words or as a prayer of thankfulness to God.

_____

_____

_____

_____

In week 2 we will dig more deeply into Satan's lies and the consequences for believing them.

To the extent that you believe these lies, the world's system influences your life.

21

Beginning a Relationship with Christ

When the goodness and love for man appeared from God our Savior, He saved us—not by works of righteousness that we had done, but according to His mercy, through the washing of regeneration and renewal by the Holy Spirit. This Spirit He poured out on us abundantly through Jesus Christ our Savior, so that having been justified by His grace we may become heirs with the hope of eternal life.

Titus 3:4-7, HCSB

Read Titus 3:4-7. Underline the words that tell us how we are saved.

We do not gain acceptance into God's eternal kingdom based on our good works. We can do no amount of good deeds—religious or otherwise—that will obligate God to save us. Salvation is a gift from God that comes to us when we accept Jesus Christ as our Savior who died for all our sins on the cross of Calvary.

Call on the Lord in repentance (literally, turn the other way from sin). Trust Him by faith as your Savior and surrender to Jesus' lordship, or rule over your life. Sincerely, using the words in the box or using similar words of your own, ask Jesus to become your Savior and Lord.

> Dear God, I know that Jesus is Your Son and that He died on the cross for me. He was raised from the dead and is a living Savior. I know that I have sinned and need forgiveness. I am willing to turn from my sins and receive Jesus as my Savior and Lord. Thank You for saving me. Amen.

If you prayed that prayer just now, welcome to the family of God. You have just made the most important decision of your life. You can be sure you are saved and have eternal life.

The moment you trust Christ, many wonderful things occur:

- All your sins—past, present, and future—are forgiven (Colossians 2:13-14).
- You become a child of God (John 1:12; Romans 8:15).
- You receive eternal life (John 5:24).
- You are delivered from Satan to the kingdom of Christ (Colossians 1:13).
- Christ comes to live in you (Revelation 3:20).God the Father has given you the Holy Spirit as a free gift when you accept Jesus Christ as Lord and Savior (1 John 3:24).
- You become a new creation (2 Corinthians 5:17).
- You are declared righteous by God (2 Corinthians 5:21).
- You enter a love relationship with God (1 John 4:9-11).

Think of how these truths apply to your life. Look up the Scriptures in your Bible. Then write a prayer in the margin thanking God for His wonderful salvation.

Week 2
Satan's Lies

NEVER GOOD ENOUGH

Brent made a list of things he could accomplish if everything went perfectly in his world that day. He became anxious if things didn't go well or if someone took too much of his time. He felt fulfilled if he used his hours efficiently and effectively. Yet even when this happened, something was missing. He felt driven to do more, but his best never was enough to satisfy him.

Brent believed that accomplishing goals and making efficient use of his time represented what the Lord wanted him to do. When he experienced stress, he occasionally thought something wasn't quite right, but his solution was to try harder, make even better use of his time, and be even more regimented.

A key verse to memorize this week:

See to it that no one takes you captive through philosophy and empty deception.
Colossians 2:8

Words to help you understand this week's lessons:

depressant (n.)—an agent that reduces one or more body functions or an instinctive desire. *(Example: Alcohol is a **depressant**.)*

stimulant (n.)—an agent that produces a temporary increase of a body function or efficiency. *(Example: Some drugs are **stimulants**.)*

This week we will discover how lies distort our self-image.
1. We believe we must meet certain standards to feel good about ourselves. That's the performance trap fed by fear of failure.
2. The second lie says we must please others in every situation. The approval addict suffers from the fear of rejection.

We will learn to identify these lies and apply what we learn to our own life situations.

Day 1
The Fear of Failure

Read again this week's verse to memorize. Paul warns us about being held captive by wrong thoughts. Most of us do not realize how completely Satan has tricked us. He has led us blindly down a path of destruction, taken us captives, and made us slaves of our low self-esteem. Satan holds us in chains that keep us from experiencing Christ's love, freedom, and purposes.

Success—No Road to Happiness

Satan has deceived many of us into believing that success will bring fulfillment and happiness. Again and again we've tried to measure up, thinking that if we could meet certain standards, we would feel good about ourselves. But again and again, we've failed and have felt miserable. Even if we succeed on a fairly regular basis, occasional failure may be so devastating that it dominates how we see ourselves.

Failure to meet these standards threatens our security and significance. Such a threat, real or imagined, results in a fear of failure. At that point we are accepting the false belief: I must meet certain standards to feel good about myself. When we believe this lie, our attitudes and behavior reflect Satan's distortion of truth.

Satan holds us in chains that keep us from experiencing Christ's love, freedom, and purposes.

Think for a moment about unrealistic standards you or someone else has set. List one standard for each category.

Job: _____

Parent: _____

Christian: _____

Spouse: _____

Friend: _____

Church: _____

How We React to Satan's Deception

Because of our unique personalities, we each react very differently to Satan's lies. Some of us respond by becoming slaves to perfectionism. We drive ourselves over and over toward reaching goals. Others of us go into a tailspin of despair. Still others withdraw from people or tasks. Let's look at how these reactions affect us.

As you read about perfectionism, despair, and withdrawal, underline key words or phrases describing the behavior. I have underlined one for you.

Perfectionism. Perfectionists may experience serious <u>mood disorders</u>. They often feel rejection is coming when they believe they haven't met standards they try hard to reach. Perfectionists tend to react defensively to criticism. They try to be in control of most situations they encounter.

Because they usually are more competent than most, perfectionists see nothing wrong with their compulsions. "I just like to see things done well." Nothing really is wrong with doing things well; the problem is that perfectionists usually base their self-worth on their ability to accomplish a goal. Failure, therefore, is a threat and totally unacceptable to them.

Karen, a wife, mother, and civic leader, seemed ideal to everyone who knew her. She was a perfectionist. Her house looked spotless, her children were perfect, and her skills as president of the Ladies' Auxiliary were superb. In each situation Karen appeared successful. However, one step out of the pattern she had set could lead to a tremendous uproar. When others failed to comply with her demands, she condemned them quickly and cruelly.

One day her husband decided that he couldn't stand any more of Karen's overly critical behavior. He wanted an understanding wife with whom he could talk and share. He didn't want a self-driven perfectionist. He wanted someone who supported him and did not condemn him when he made some inevitable mistake. Friends could not understand why this husband chose to leave his "perfect" wife. Like Karen, many high achievers are driven beyond healthy limitations. They can rarely relax and enjoy life because they're constantly striving toward some accomplishment. Their families and relationships suffer as they try to achieve unrealistic goals.

Despair and passivity. On the other hand, the same false belief (I must meet certain standards to feel good about myself) drives

Behold, You desire truth in the innermost being, and in the hidden part You will make me know wisdom.
Psalm 51:6

25

others to despair. They rarely expect to achieve anything or to feel good about themselves. Because they have failed in the past, they believe their present failures only show how worthless they really are. They often become extremely sad and stop trying because they fear more failure.

Withdrawal. Those who show this behavior usually sidestep risks by trying to avoid failure and disapproval. They won't volunteer for the jobs that offer much risk of failure. They move toward people who are comforting and kind. They skirt relationships that might make them vulnerable and that consequently might cause them to risk rejection. They may appear to be easygoing, but inside they usually are running from every possible situation or relationship that might not succeed.

Think of a situation in which your performance did not measure up to the standard you had set for yourself. What thoughts and emotions arose because of that situation? What action did you take in response to those emotions? Read the example below; then write your thoughts.

Example:
Situation: I was late to an appointment.
Standard: I must be on time.
Thoughts: I'm always late. I try, but I just can't be on time. I'm so ashamed of myself.
Emotions: Anger, depression
Actions: I blamed being late on my wife and daughter.

Situation: _____

Standard: _____

Thoughts: _____

Emotions: _____

> **In almost any activity or relationship, perfectionists will likely experience the fear of failure.**

In almost any activity or relationship, perfectionists will likely experience the fear of failure. When they fail, they usually feel:

Anger	Fear
Resentment	Anxiety
Worry	Depression

In turn, these emotions express themselves through actions like:

Impatience	Rudeness
Hostility	Blaming

As we close today's study, start to memorize the first two lines of the affirmation "My Identity in Christ." Also begin memorizing this week's Scripture.

Day 2
A Rules~Dominated Life

The pressure of having to meet self-imposed standards to feel good about ourselves can cause a person to live a rules-dominated life. Individuals caught in this trap continually focus their attention on their performance and on their ability to stick to their rules.

Three years after Pam married, she committed adultery with a coworker. Although she had confessed her sin to God and to her husband and had been forgiven, guilt continued to plague her. She found that it was difficult for her to feel acceptable to God.

Four years after the affair, she still could not forgive herself for what she had done. Sitting in my office, we explored her reluctance to accept God's forgiveness. "It sounds as though you believe that God can't forgive the sin you committed," I said. "That's right," she replied. "I don't think He ever will."
"But God doesn't base His love and acceptance of us on our performance," I said. "If any sin is so filthy and vile that it makes us less acceptable to Him, then the cross is insufficient. If the cross isn't sufficient for all sin, then the Bible is in error when it says that He forgave all your sins (Colossians 2:13-15). God also took away Satan's power to condemn us for sin."

As this case demonstrates, the false belief—I must meet certain standards to feel good about myself—results in a fear of failure. How much does this belief affect you? Try to be objective to determine how strongly you fear failure.

Cutting Yourself Off
When our performance meets our standard, it can give a sense of pride that we might mistake for self-worth. We feel good; we feel significant. We then strive to meet another standard and then another so we can continue to feel good about ourselves. We use performance to evaluate our self-worth because the system reinforces itself: when we perform well, we feel good. This success makes us feel that the system works, so we keep using it.

Try to be objective to determine how strongly you fear failure.

Please note: it isn't wrong to be glad we succeeded at something. The issue is whether we base our self-worth on succeeding. Our performance leads us to pride and/or insecurity. God's truth leads us to true joy and the desire to honor Him in all things.

If we reject God's provision for self-worth and instead embrace the world's false promises, our performance is our only alternative for meeting this deep need. We usually act according to our beliefs. If you believe you are a failure, you may cut yourself off from a worthwhile activity because you fear you will fail at it.

Another way we might have coped with this fear of failure was to drive ourselves to succeed to prove that we're not a failure. Again, our performance often reflects our belief system. If our belief system is based on false beliefs, then our thoughts, emotions, and actions usually will reflect those false beliefs.

By now you have memorized the first false belief and probably are beginning to learn the second one. Review by turning to the inside back cover for help. Write here the first false belief.

I must meet certain _____

Day 3

Effects of the Fear of Failure

How the Fear of Failure Affects Our Lives
The following list does not represent all of the problems that result from the fear of failure. Neither does the fear of failure explain why all of these problems occur. However, recognizing the symptoms in each of these examples could change your life.

Recognizing the symptoms of fear of failure could change your life.

Perfectionism
On page 25 we read about perfectionism. It affects us by suffocating joy and creativity. We tend to focus our attention on the failure rather than on our successes, because we consider any failure as a threat to our self-esteem. We tend to be perfectionists about such issues as work, being on time, house cleaning, our appearance, hobbies, and skills. Perfectionists often appear to be highly motivated or driven, but their motivations usually come from a desperate attempt to avoid the pain of failure.

Avoiding Risks

In addition to perfectionism, fear of failure affects us in another way. We choose to be involved in only those activities we can do well. We avoid challenging activities. Avoiding risks may seem comfortable, but it severely limits the scope of our creativity, self-expression, and service to God.

Anger, Resentment

Anger is a normal response when we fail, when others contribute to our failure, or when we are injured or insulted in some way. Feeling angry isn't wrong. In fact, the apostle Paul encouraged the Ephesians to be angry, but he also quickly warned them not to express anger in a sinful, hurtful way, as the verse in the margin shows. Unfortunately, rather than using our anger in a helpful way, many of us either vent our fury without thinking about how it affects people or hold our anger inside. Anger held inside eventually leads to outbursts in which we "get back" at people. We may also feel deep and seething resentment and/or depression.

> Be angry, and yet do not sin; do not let the sun go down on your anger.
> Ephesians 4:26

Choose one of these three problems resulting from the fear of failure. How does it affect your life?

_____

_____

_____

Anxiety

Failure often causes us to condemn ourselves and causes others to disapprove of us. If our self-worth is based on personal success and approval, such disapproval deals us a severe blow. If failure is great enough or occurs often enough, it can harden into a negative self-concept in which we expect to fail at almost everything we try. This negative self-concept goes on continually and leads to a downward spiral of anxiety about our performance and fear of disapproval from others.

Pride

When we base our self-worth on our performance and succeed in that performance, we often develop an inflated view of ourselves. This inflated view is pride. Some of us may keep up this wrongful pride through any and all circumstances. For most of us, however, this sense of self-esteem lasts only until our next failure (or risk of failure). Pride gives us a false front to hide our fear.

Being proud of an accomplishment is good. This feeling is not the same as an inflated ego trip in which we appear better than we are, nor does it produce negative self-doubts.

Depression

Depression generally results when a person turns anger inward and/or feels a deep sense of loss. Experiencing failure and fearing future failing can lead to deep depression. Once depressed, many people become emotionally numb or unfeeling. They begin to act passively, lacking energy or will. They believe they have no hope for change. Generally, depression is the body's way of blocking the mind's pain. It does this by numbing physical and emotional functions.

Depression is the body's way of blocking the mind's pain.

Describe a time in which you felt the results of fear of failure because of perfectionism, anxiety, or depression.

_____

_____

_____

Low Motivation

Many people who seem lazy or who have low motivation actually feel hopeless. If people believe they will fail, they have no reason to put forth any effort. The pain they endure for their passivity seems relatively minor and acceptable compared to the agony of genuinely trying and failing.

Sexual Dysfunction

The emotional trauma failure causes can disturb sexual activity in marriage. Then, rather than experiencing the pain of failing sexually, many people tend to avoid sexual activity altogether.

Chemical Dependency

Many people attempt to ease their pain and fear of failure by drinking. Those who abuse alcohol often do so with the false idea that it will cause them to perform at a greater level and will make them more likely to succeed. However, alcohol and other drugs are **depressants,** making the person less likely to perform well.

People often use other types of drugs called **stimulants,** because they believe these will make them more productive. People who use these drugs likely consume larger doses until the users are addicted.

Chemical substances are addictive and easily abused. Drug binges cause bodily resources to be depleted, so that when users come down from the chemical's high effect, they crash. Individuals may have started using these substances as a way to escape from their troubles temporarily. They also may have thought using these substances would remove pressures to perform.

However, when the substance's effect wears off, these individuals realize in despair that they can't cope without the substance. This pain-pleasure cycle continues, slowly draining the life from its victim. Cocaine users represent a clear example of this truth. One reason cocaine is popular is that it produces feelings of greater self-esteem. Why would cocaine be necessary if the false self-esteem they feel is quite enough for them? They would not be seeking more.

How would your life be different if you did not experience the fear of failure?

Day 4
Driven to Please People

The second of Satan's lies preys on what others think about us. As a result, the need for approval can drive us to insane lengths to receive affirmation.

Randy felt like a vending machine. Anyone wanting something could pull an invisible lever and get it. On the job Randy was always doing other people's work for them. At home his friends continually called on him to help them with odd jobs. His wife insisted that he hold down outside employment so that they could live an affluent life-style. Even people in Randy's church took advantage of him. They knew they could count on good old Randy to direct a number of the programs they planned. He said yes until he was exhausted.

What was the problem? Was Randy simply a self-sacrificing saint, or did his inability to say no stem from his fear of rejection?

Whom have I in heaven but You? And besides You, I desire nothing on earth. But as for me, the nearness of God is my good; I have made the Lord GOD my refuge, that I may tell of all Your works.

Psalm 73:25,28

31

Randy deeply resented those people who demanded so much from him and left him with little time for himself. Yet he just couldn't refuse. He longed for others' approval, and he feared their rejection. He believed that by agreeing to their every wish, he would win their approval and would make sure they did not shut him out.

Randy typifies many of us. We spend much of our time building relationships and striving to win others' respect. We give of ourselves to the point of exhaustion because we feel that doing so will make people appreciate us and avoid rejection.

Describe a time when you've acted like Randy. You said yes to too many requests and worked yourself to exhaustion because you wanted someone's approval and feared that person's rejection.

_____

_____

_____

Whose approval do you need and whose rejection do you fear?

How Others' Expectations Affect Me

Let's personalize today's lesson a bit by looking at some persons whose approval you need and whose rejection you fear. Only when we study how this situation works in our own lives can we begin to understand why it happens and what we can do about it.

List below names of persons whose approval you need and whose rejection you fear. These individuals might include your parents, boyfriend/girlfriend, spouse, peer group, or boss. Even God might be on your list.

_____   _____

_____   _____

_____   _____

What Rejection Feels Like

Why do we fear rejection so greatly? How does rejection show itself in our lives? What does it communicate to us? You can probably list more than one occasion in which you've experienced rejection. This rejection may have occurred in a subtle, indirect, or even nonverbal manner. For example, you may have felt it in a friend's disgusted look, an individual's snub after you say hello, a coworker who rudely keeps his eye on his computer screen for minutes after you've entered his office, or a general icy coolness that you detect when you enter a room.

Think of situations in which someone has communicated rejection by a facial expression or behavior. Draw a picture in the margin or describe it here.

_____

Other times you may have felt rejected in more direct ways. For example, you may have felt it in a professor's sarcastic remark about your paper, a potential employer's don't-call-us; we'll-call-you letter, a group's excluding you from a function, an athletic team's choosing you last, or an impatient answer.

Virtually all of us fear rejection. We can fall prey to it even when we've learned to harden our defenses as we anticipate someone's disapproval. Neither being defensive nor trying to please another person at all costs is the answer to this problem. These approaches to our fear of rejection actually prevent us from dealing with that fear's root cause. They also keep us from being all God intended.

The following results of approval addiction are not exhaustive but designed to demonstrate how the fear of rejection can affect many areas of our lives.

Inability to Give and Receive Love
One result of our fear of rejection is that we become unable to give and receive love. We find it difficult to open up and reveal our inner thoughts and needs because we believe others will reject us if they know what we're *really* like.

Beloved, if God so loved us, we also ought to love one another.
1 John 4:11

Michael, for example, was reared in a broken home. Michael's father had been given custody of the boy, although he did not want it. Michael's mother was too busy with her whirl of social activities to care for him. Later Michael's father married another woman who had three children. This new wife and her children began to resent Michael.

When Michael grew up and married a wonderful woman who truly loved him, he was cautious about sharing his love with her, because he had experienced the pain of rejection all his life.

Because of that rejection he withheld his love from someone he truly cared for because he was afraid of becoming too close. His parents had rejected him, and if his wife rejected him as they had done, the pain would be too much for him to bear.

Describe a time in which you did not reveal your inner self because you feared rejection.

_____

_____

Avoiding People
Some people react to their fear of rejection by avoiding others, thereby avoiding the risk that they'll be rejected. Some people avoid others and spend most of their time alone, while others deal with this fear by having numerous relationships but keeping them on the surface. They may know how to make friends easily and seem outgoing, but their friendships never are deep ones. Their friends never really get to know them because these people hide behind a wall of words, smiles, and activities. These people usually are quite lonely in the midst of all their "friends."

Do these words describe you? ❏ Yes ❏ No
Have you avoided people to avoid the risk that they would reject you? ❏ Yes ❏ No

Bowing to Peer Pressure
Fear of rejection causes us to bow to peer pressure in an effort to gain approval. We may join clubs and organizations, hoping we'll be accepted. We may identify ourselves with social groups, believing that being with these groups will ensure our acceptance and their approval.

Experimenting with Drugs or Sex
Many people admit that they bow to peer pressure for fear that they won't be accepted if they don't. However, drugs and sexual promiscuity promise something they can't fulfill. Experimenting only leaves these people with pain. It also leaves them with a deeper need for self-worth and acceptance.

Allowing Others to Influence Our Moral Standards
Some of us have established our moral standards based on the approval or disapproval of others. Rather than letting God speak to us through His Word as our authority on matters of life, we have referred to people, doing what they approve of or encourage

Do you not know that your body is a temple of the Holy Spirit who is in you, whom you have from God, and that you are not your own? For you have been bought with a price; therefore glorify God in your body.
1 Corinthians 6:19-20

us to do. This may have led some of us to compromise our sexual purity, moral and ethical integrity, and our walk with God.

Based on the results we've studied so far, check below the ways you can see the fear of rejection in your life.

- ❏ I have difficulty giving and receiving love.
- ❏ I avoid people.
- ❏ I bow to peer pressure.
- ❏ I have experimented with drugs or sex.
- ❏ I allow others to influence my moral standards.
- ❏ These words do not describe me.

We experience the fear of rejection and its accompanying problems because we believe Satan's lie that our self-worth = performance + others' opinions. We crave love, fellowship, and intimacy, and we turn to others to meet those needs. However, the problem with basing our worth on the approval of others is that only God loves and appreciates us without conditions. He has provided a solution to the approval addiction.

Be of sober spirit, be on the alert. Your adversary, the devil, prowls around like a roaring lion, seeking someone to devour.

1 Peter 5:8

Fill in the blanks to review Satan's first two lies:

I must meet certain _____ to feel good about myself.

I must be _____ by certain others to feel good about myself.

Day 5
The Hazards Go On

As if the hazards we read about in day 4 weren't enough, the list goes on. Day 5 contains four other reactions.

Other Reactions to the Fear of Rejection

Feeling Manipulated
Those who believe their self-worth is based on others' approval likely will do just about anything to please people. They truly believe that they will be well liked if they comply with the requests of others. Many end up despising those who manipulate them and resent what they feel they have to do for others' approval.

Praise can be a form of manipulation.

Sometimes people praise us to help us, build us up, and encourage us, but praise can be a form of manipulation. Some people use praise to get us to accomplish their goals, to contribute to their program, or to help them look good in front of others. In that sense, praise is a subtle but powerful form of rejection. Unfortunately, many of us fall prey to this harmful, manipulative praise because we so desperately want appreciation.

> **Check below the response(s) you feel when people praise you only to manipulate you.**
> ❏ I feel used, like an object.
> ❏ I resent being used.
> ❏ I get angry with the person.

If you see that someone is praising you only to manipulate you, then you very well may feel used, like an object instead of a person. You may feel very angry at the person. People who manipulate us with praise are using us as tools to accomplish their goals while they reject us as people. A kind of sickness of spirit may settle on us. Do we really need others' approval so much that we'll tolerate this treatment?

Need to Be in Control of All Situations
In their fear of rejection and in their efforts to avoid being hurt, many people constantly try to maintain control of others and dominate most situations. Greg needed to control so much that he refused to attend parties unless he was the host. If coworkers needed five minutes of his time to discuss a project, he was too busy. Yet Greg showed up frequently in coworkers' offices unannounced and demanded their uninterrupted time, even if it was inconvenient for them.

Such people are skilled in controlling by giving out approval or disapproval. They are unwilling to let others be themselves and to make their own decisions without their consent. People who fear rejection are so insecure that the thought of not controlling every situation horrifies them.

Defensiveness
Our fear of rejection makes us run from any type of open discussion of issues. Fred always bristled and found an excuse to avoid meeting when members of the church committee he chaired approached him with a concern. Instead of making possible an honest, helpful talk, Fred went on the defensive immediately. He feared rejection so much he ran from any situation in which he thought he might feel pain.

Passivity

We may become passive because of our fear of rejection. We may withdraw by avoiding decisions and activities in which we might be criticized. We also avoid activities in which we can't be sure we'll be successful. Our goal in these instances usually is to avoid the pain of rejection by not doing anything that might be objectionable. This also prevents us from enjoying the pleasures of healthy relationships and achievements.

Based on the results we've studied in this lesson, check the ways you can see the fear of rejection in your life.

- ❏ I allow others to manipulate me.
- ❏ I feel that I must be in control.
- ❏ I become defensive.
- ❏ I avoid the pain of rejection by not participating.
- ❏ These choices do not describe me.

If you checked one of the effects, what emotions do you feel in such situations?

_____

_____

All of us need to grow in our self-concept, in our relationships with God, and in our relationships with others.

Can I Ever Be Completely Free?

Probably not. It may be impossible for us to totally shed our need for others' approval and our fear of rejection. You may be surprised to learn this. Perhaps you assume that reading this book and completing its exercises will keep you forever from basing your self-worth on what others think of you.

I don't believe that any of us will gain complete freedom from this tendency until we're with the Lord someday. Our God-given instinct to survive compels us to avoid pain. Knowing that rejection and disapproval bring pain, we will continue our attempts to win the esteem of others whenever possible. In week 5 we will learn ways to grow in our relationship with God so that He is the One whose approval means most to us.

Whether, then, you eat or drink or whatever you do, do all to the glory of God.

1 Corinthians 10:31

Week 3
God's Truth

WRONG REASONING

Phillip was reared in a strict church family. He was taught that cursing is a terrible sin. All of Phillip's friends cursed, but he never did. He secretly thought that he was better than his friends. Phillip never acted based on what God wanted or because of God's love for him. Instead, he acted because he was determined to live up to his standards. Phillip needed to base his behavior on God and His Word, not on his own standards.

Brian attended church because he thought doing so would cause God to bless his business, not because he wanted to worship God. Cheryl told God she wouldn't spread gossip about Diane if He would get her the raise she wanted. What do Phillip, Brian, and Cheryl need to know about God and His truth?

A key verse to memorize this week:

Having been justified by faith, we have peace with God through our Lord Jesus Christ.

Romans 5:1

Words to help you understand this week's lessons:

justified (v.)—placed in right standing before God through Christ's death on the cross, which paid for our sins. *(Example: We have been **justified** freely through the death of Jesus Christ.)*

righteousness (n.)—a characteristic of God, meaning essentially the same as His faithfulness or truthfulness. We have right standing with God through Christ. *(Example: God didn't stop with just forgiving us; He credited to us the very **righteousness** of Christ.)*

repentance (n.)—a change of mind that involves both a turning from sin and a turning to God. *(Example: Satan tries to make us believe that reliving sin to punish ourselves for it is part of **repentance**.)*

This week we will examine Scriptures that assure us of our unique place in God's plan. God has given us a secure self-worth totally apart from our ability to perform or to measure up to others. I hope you will be encouraged to know how much God loves you as His precious child—just the way you are. God has revealed His good, acceptable, and perfect will for our lives in His Word, and we must learn to embrace and apply His truth and refuse to believe Satan's lies.

We must learn to embrace and apply God's truth and refuse to believe Satan's lies.

Day 1
The Source of Truth

Before we move on, let's review the first seven lines of "My Identity in Christ." Fill in the blanks.

Because of Christ's _____, I am a new creation of infinite worth.

I am deeply _____, I am completely

_____, I am fully _____.

I am totally _____ by God.

I am absolutely complete in _____.

If we base our self-worth on false beliefs, we will try to find it by avoiding risks or by trying to succeed no matter what the cost. Either way, failure looms as a constant enemy. God's truth is the only reality that can help our thinking to be conformed to His, so that our self-esteem is based on how He values us.

When I Was a Teenager ...

As I reflect on my life, I recall that I especially feared failure during my teenage years. This fear was apparent particularly in athletics.

During those years I practiced basketball a lot and became a good player. In the process I learned that I could attempt many maneuvers while I practiced on the court or while I played basketball with friends, but during a game when I felt intense pressure, I was afraid to do those same maneuvers. I now realize that same fear has prevented me from attempting things in several other areas of my life. Although God has enabled me on many occasions to conquer this fear, I still struggle with the risk of failing.

People who have achieved a level of competence know that after they have been successful, they also continue to fear losing this ability. Success does not necessarily reduce the amount of fear we experience in our lives. In fact, success often causes us to have even more fear because we feel that we have more to lose.

God's Solution

Spread the good news! God has not given up on us. Thankfully, God has a solution for the fear of failure. He has given us a secure self-worth totally apart from our ability to perform. We have been **justified.**

They are justified freely by His grace through the redemption that is in Christ Jesus.

Romans 3:24, HCSB

Read Romans 3:24 in the margin. How did God accomplish justification for us? Write Y (yes) or N (no) for each statement.

_____ I am justified by my words and lifestyle.
_____ I am justified because people love me.
_____ I am justified because I try harder than most people to lead a good life.
_____ I am justified by God's grace through Christ's redemption on the cross.

How do you feel when you realize the truth of this verse— that you are justified by faith? Write several feeling words in the margin.

The fact that you are justified is one of God's truths that you can use to reject the fear of failure or disapproval. As you reject these false beliefs you can replace them with confidence that God has transferred all your sin to Jesus Christ and has given you His righteousness. That's what happens in justification. Read the first of God's truths that we are going to affirm in this week's study:

He made the One who did not know sin to be sin for us, so that we might become the righteousness of God in Him.

2 Corinthians 5:21

> Because of justification, I am completely forgiven by and fully pleasing to God. I no longer have to fear failure.

Visualize two ledgers: On one is a list of all your sins; on the other, the righteousness of Christ. Now exchange your ledger for Christ's. This exchange transfers your sin to Christ and His righteousness to you.

I once heard a radio preacher criticize members of his congregation for their hidden sins. He exclaimed, "Don't you know that someday you're going to die and God is going to flash all your sins on a giant screen in heaven for all the world to see?" This minister misunderstood God's gracious gift of justification! Justification carries with it no guilt. By dying on the cross, Christ paid for all of our sins—past, present, and future. God forgives us completely!

Check the statements below that indicate the results of justification.

❏ Because of justification God forgives your sin and does not hold it against you.
❏ You have peace with God. You no longer are considered His enemy.
❏ You are saved from His wrath.
❏ You do not have to fear condemnation.
❏ You can now live to honor Him and to reflect His image.
❏ You are declared righteous.
❏ You are an heir of His eternal kingdom.

Christ's Righteousness

As marvelous as justification is, it means more than forgiveness of sins. In the same act of love through which God forgave us, He also provided the **righteousness** to stand in God's presence. I hope you checked all of the boxes in the last activity.

Suppose you and Christ were seated next to each other, and someone asked God, the Father, "Which of these two persons do You love the most? Which person is more acceptable to You? Which person is holy and blameless before You?" God the Father would respond, "They are equally loved in My sight."

In a prayer to God, thank Him for His love. Tell God how much you love Him in return.

Day 2
Forgiven, Fully Pleasing

God intended for Adam and his descendants to be righteous people. He intended for them to experience fully His love and His purposes for them. But sin short-circuited that relationship. God's perfect payment for sin—the death of His Son—has satisfied the righteous wrath of God. This new relationship delights God and enables us to know and honor the Lord.

Much more them, having now been justified by His blood, we shall be saved from the wrath of God through Him.

Romans 5:9

According to the Law, one may almost say, all things are cleansed with blood, and without shedding of blood there is no forgiveness. ... "and their sins and their lawless deeds I will remember no more."

Hebrews 9:22; 10:17

41

The Reality of Righteousness

If you've trusted in Christ's death on the cross for forgiveness of your sins, God has declared you to be righteous in His sight. To God, our worth does not depend on our performance. You may be thinking, *I was never really that bad*. But to God even your best attempts at righteousness were as filthy rags (Isaiah 64:6). But take heart! God has seen your helplessness. He has extended justification to you through Christ's death and resurrection.

The Realities of Redemption

Mark the following statements as T (true) or F (false).

_____ Reliving past sin to punish myself is part of repentance (see p. 38).

_____ Reliving past sin to punish myself is a way of paying for my sin.

_____ Reliving past sin to punish myself is unnecessary and harmful to my self-worth in Christ.

_____ Reliving past sin to punish myself is a way to control my future actions.

Being aware of sin is a crucial element of repentance. However, our wrongful thinking goes like this: *By reliving this sin in order to punish myself, I inflict pain upon myself. That pain will become associated with these sins so I never will do them again. Therefore, remembering sin is helpful and good.*

Why does recalling these sins cause pain? Each time you remember them, you judge yourself according to your poor past performance. The evaluation always comes out negative, and the pain of self-hatred follows. If you were not evaluating yourself by your past performance, you probably would not dredge up the painful memory of these sins.

Their sins and their lawless deeds
I will remember no more.
Hebrews 10:17

Read Hebrews 10:17. Reliving sin is a destructive way of trying to produce a godly life. God's method is to forgive our sins. Ask God to enable you to accept His forgiveness.

If we have trusted in Christ for our salvation, we each can say with certainty this statement from "My Identity in Christ"(p. 113):

I am deeply loved, completely forgiven, fully pleasing, and totally accepted by God. I am absolutely complete in Christ.

Think for a minute about what you just read. Review the key verse for this week (p. 38). Write the word that tells how we are justified. Then, write the result of justification.

_____   _____

You can do nothing to add to or to take away from what Christ did for you on the cross. Although you may try to justify yourself by doing good deeds to show God that you deserve your justification, it is a vain attempt to gain what you already have. Your new life is a product of God's workmanship in which He is very pleased. As this truth renews your mind, you increasingly will reflect this in your attitudes and behavior (see Romans 12:1-2).

Am I Really Pleasing to God?
Some people have difficulty thinking of themselves as being pleasing to God because they link pleasing so strongly with performance. They tend to be displeased with anything short of perfection in themselves, and they suspect that God has the same standard.

The point of justification is that we never can achieve perfection on this earth. Even our best efforts at self-righteousness are as filthy garments to God Isaiah 64:6). Yet He loves us so much that He appointed His Son to pay for our sins. Christ credited to us His perfect status before God.

Right Motivations
Understanding our complete forgiveness and acceptance before God does not mean we should have a casual attitude toward sin. On the contrary, understanding what it cost God gives us a greater desire to serve the One who died to free us from the control of sin. I am not minimizing the destructive nature of sin, but I am trying to make sure we see Christ's payment on the cross as sufficient.

If good works won't make a person more pleasing to God, why should a person be involved in good works? Justification doesn't mean that actions don't matter and that we can sin all we want. God hates sin. Our sinful actions, words, and attitudes grieve the Lord, but our status as beloved children remains intact. In His love He disciplines and encourages us to live godly lives—both for our good and for His honor.

In Romans 6:12-13, 1 Corinthians 6:18-20, Colossians 3:23-24, Titus 2:11-14, and other passages Paul strongly stated his desire to please and glorify the One who had credited to him Christ's righteousness.

Understanding our complete forgiveness and acceptance before God does not mean we should have a casual attitude toward sin.

43

Based on your reading of these Scriptures, mark the statements below as T (true) or F (false).

_____ People are to offer themselves to God for service.

_____ People are to honor God with their bodies.

_____ People are to work at everything as if they are working for the Lord.

_____ People are to daily be on the lookout for good deeds they can perform.

_____ People are to deny themselves of ungodliness and worldly desires.

All the statements in the above exercise are true. As you are more and more aware of what God has done for you, your natural response will be to honor Him in your daily life.

Day 3

Motivations for Obedience

Right Things for Right Reasons

Are you doing the right things for the right reasons? What determines whether a deed will honor God?

Check the following statements that affirm what the Scriptures say about whether a deed will honor God.

❏ Deeds can come from a person's faith.

❏ Deeds can be done to help people.

❏ Deeds can be done for the glory of God.

❏ Deeds can to be done to impress people.

❏ Deeds can be done to cause a person to owe me for what I have done for them.

Six Reasons to Obey God

The love of God and His acceptance of us are based on grace. But if He accepts us on the basis of His grace and not because of our deeds, why should we obey God? Here are six good reasons to obey Him. We will study the first three today and the last three in day 4.

Christ's Love

When we experience love, we usually respond by seeking to express our love in return. Obeying God is a way we show our love for Him, which comes from an understanding of what Christ

Prove yourselves doers of the word, and not merely hearers who delude themselves. For if anyone is a hearer of the word and not a doer, he is like a man who looks at his natural face in a mirror; for once he has looked at himself and gone away, he has immediately forgotten what kind of person he was. But one who looks intently at the perfect law, the law of liberty, and abides by it, not having become a forgetful hearer but an effectual doer, this man will be blessed in what he does.

James 1: 22-25

Little children, let us not love with word or with tongue, but in deed and truth. We will know by this that we are of the truth, and will assure our heart before Him.

1 John 3:18-19

has accomplished for us on the cross (2 Corinthians 5:14-15). We love because He first loved us and clearly demonstrated His love for us at the cross (1 John 4:16-19). Understanding this love highly motivates us to serve Him.

Our experience of God's love is based on a belief. If we believe that He is demanding or faraway and disinterested, we will not be able to receive His love and tenderness. Instead, we either will be afraid of Him or angry with Him. Faulty views of God often prompt us to rebel against Him.

Think of occasions when you have withdrawn from God or have been angry with Him and rebellious against Him. Circle actions that grew out of that belief.

Disobedience   Lying   Prayerlessness   Apathy
Selfishness   Hostility   Worldly

Other: _____

Read the Scriptures in the margin. Answer the following questions (Y) yes or (N) no, based on what you read.

_____ Did Christ die for us while we were still sinners?
_____ Did God send His Son because He loved everyone?
_____ Did God sacrifice His Son because of His great love for you?
_____ Does your love of Christ lead you to obey Him?

How we see God forms all of our motivations. As we grow in understanding His unconditional love and acceptance, we will better grasp that He disciples us because He cares, not because He's cruel. We will be able to see the contrast between the joys of living for Christ and the destructive nature of sin.

Sin's Destruction

Sin is destructive in many ways. Emotionally, sin causes us to experience the pain of guilt and shame and the fear of failure and punishment. Mentally, sin causes us to experience the anguish of flashbacks—continuing to relive our sin. We also may spend enormous amounts of time and energy thinking about our sins and trying to explain away our guilt. Physically, sin may cause us to suffer from psychosomatic illnesses or to experience pain through physical abuse. Sin also may result in the loss of property or even the loss of life. Relationally, sin separates us from others.

God so loved the world, that He gave His only begotten Son, that whoever believes in Him should not perish, but have eternal life. For God did not send the Son into the world to judge the world, but that the world might be saved through Him.

John 3:16-18

While we were still helpless, at the right time Christ died for the ungodly. For one will hardly die for a righteous man; though perhaps for the good man someone would dare even to die. But God demonstrates His own love toward us, in that while we were yet sinners, Christ died for us.

Romans 5:6-8

The Bible character Jonah is known for his disobedience. Check the statements below that give the results of Jonah's choice of disobedience to God.

❑ Jonah's sin endangered the lives of those around him.
❑ Jonah was able to continue doing as he pleased.
❑ Jonah involved others in his sin.
❑ Jonah was isolated from God and others.

Satan has blinded us to the painful, damaging consequences of sin. The effects of sin are all around us, yet many people continue to indulge in sins such as pride and self-centeredness, status and pleasure seeking, and independence from God, which causes Him much anguish and pain.

Satan contradicted God in the garden when he said, "You surely will not die!" (Genesis 3:4). Sin may seem pleasant but does so only for a while. Sooner or later, sin will cause some form of destruction. Emotionally, it will separate us from others.

Spiritually, sin causes us to make the Holy Spirit sad, to lose our testimony, and to break our fellowship with God. The painful and destructive effects of sin are so profound that it is a mystery why we don't have an intense dislike for it.

The Father's Discipline

Read Hebrews 12:5-11 in your Bible. Mark the following statements as T (true) or F (false), based on these verses.

_____ God disciplines us because He truly loves us.
_____ Discipline is proof that we have become the children of God.
_____ God disciplines us in love and never punishes us in anger.
_____ God disciplines us because we aren't perfect.

Our loving Father has given us the Holy Spirit to convict us of sin. Conviction is a form of God's discipline and serves as proof that we have become sons of God (Hebrews 12:5-11). It warns us that we are making choices without regard either to God's truth or sin's consequences. If we choose not to respond to the Holy Spirit, our Heavenly Father will discipline us in love.

Note the differences between punishment and discipline.

Punishment	Discipline
God's wrath	God's love
To avenge a wrong	To correct a wrong
Alienation	Recognition
Guilt	A righteous lifestyle
Nonbelievers	His children

Most of us equate discipline with punishment. This misunderstanding of God's intentions causes us to fear God rather than to respond to His love. We no longer need to fear punishment from God for our sins. We can seek to do what is right knowing that when He disciplines us, we can remember that God is correcting us in love. This discipline leads us to righteous living, which reflects Christ's righteousness in us.

In the margin write about a time in the past when you understood that God was correcting you in love.

Day 4
More Reasons for Obedience

In day 3 we examined three good reasons for obeying God: Christ's love, sin's destruction, and the Father's discipline. Today we will study three more: His good commands, eternal rewards, and Christ' worthiness.

His Good Commands

Read Romans 7:12 and 1 John 5:3. Then complete the statement that follows these verses.

God's commands are described as _____,

_____ , _____

and not _____ .

God gives His commands to us for two good purposes:

* to protect us from sin's destructiveness and
* to direct us in a life of joy and fruitfulness.

The Law is holy, and the commandment is holy and righteous and good.
Romans 7:12

This is the love of God, that we keep His commandments; and His commandments are not burdensome.

1 John 5:3

47

If we believe that our worth is secure in Christ, then we will view His commands as helpful guidelines.

Most of us have a negative attitude about God's commands. If we believe that our worth is based on our performance, then every command is just one more thing we have to do to earn our acceptance. But if we believe that our worth is secure in Christ, then we will view His commands as helpful guidelines.

We have a wrong perspective if we view God's commands only as restrictions in our lives. Instead, we must realize that His commands are guidelines, given so that we might enjoy life to the fullest.

God's commands are holy, right, and good; and the Holy Spirit gives us the wisdom and strength to keep them. Therefore, since these commands have value in themselves, we can choose to obey God and follow His commands.

Write one of God's commands. Then explain why it is given for our benefit.

_____

_____

_____

Eternal Rewards

Through Christ's payment for us on the cross, we have escaped eternal judgment; however, our actions will be judged when we appear before Christ at the judgment seat. He will reward us for deeds that reflected a desire to honor Christ. However, He will reject deeds that dishonored Christ.

I have fought the good fight, I have finished the course, I have kept the faith; in the future there is laid up for me the crown of righteousness, which the Lord, the righteous Judge, will award to me on that day; and not only to me, but also to all who have loved His appearing.

2 Timothy 4:7-8

Read 2 Timothy 4:7-8 in the margin. Match the correct answers with the following questions.

___1. How should we run the race of life?

___2. How do you get the victor's crown?

___3. What is in store for a Christian?

A. By righteousness

B. A prize

C. By competing

Although we do not become more acceptable to God because of our rewards, our rewards represent our faithful service to Him. Rewards, then, are an honor God gives us because we have honored Him.

Christ's Worthiness

Our most noble motivation for serving Christ is that He is worthy of our love and obedience. Christ deserves our affection and obedience. No other person, no goal, no fame or status, and no material possession can compare with Him. The more we understand His love and majesty, the more we will praise Him and desire to honor Him at the expense of everything else.

Using these passages, write a brief purpose statement for your life.

> Do you not know that you are a temple of God, and that the Spirit of God dwells in you? If any man destroys the temple of God, God will destroy him, for the temple of God is holy, and that is what you are.
>
> 1 Corinthians 3:16-17

> You are a chosen race, a royal priesthood, a holy nation, a people for God's own possession, that you may proclaim the excellencies of Him who has called you out of darkness into His marvelous light.
>
> 1 Peter 2:9

_____

_____

You are to reflect Christ's image through the way you live and to proclaim the great things about Him to those around you.

Here are the six reasons to obey God. Check the top three that motivate you.

_____ He is worthy of our obedience.
_____ Christ's love motivates us to live for Him.
_____ Sin is destructive and should be avoided.
_____ Our Father lovingly disciplines us for wrongdoing.
_____ His commands for us are good.
_____ We will receive eternal rewards for obedience.

Usually, the motivations to honor God and to express our love for Him are higher because they focus on Christ and represent a response to His love and majesty. Simple and pure devotion to Christ is our highest and best motivation for serving Him. Justification carries with it no guilt. God forgives us completely!

Simple and pure devotion to Christ is our highest and best motivation for serving Him.

Think about an area of your life in which you need motivation to obey Christ more. Write about that area on the lines below.

_____

_____

_____

Stop and pray, asking God's guidance in the area of your life you mentioned that needs concentration. Ask your prayer partner to pray with you about this area of need (see p. 11).

Ask God to help you see what steps of obedience to Him you need to take.

Day 5
Poor Reasons for Obedience

Why Do We Obey?
Now we'll turn to some reasons for obeying God that aren't the best. Jesus said over and over that He cared about not only what we do but also why we do it. The Pharisees (the margin tells more about who they were) obeyed many rules and regulations, but their hearts were far from the Lord. Motives are important. The following are some poor motivations for obeying God and their possible results.

1. Someone May Find Out
Many people obey God because they are afraid of what others will think of them if they don't obey. Allen visited prospects for his church because he feared what his Sunday School class would think if he didn't go.

You will have many problems if you let what others think determine how you behave. To begin with, sometimes no one is watching. The motive to stay away from sin is missing, so you indulge in it. Sometimes you may decide you want to disobey more than you want to please or more than you want to avoid offending others. Finally, once someone has found out you've sinned, you no longer have a reason to obey.

Pharisees (n.)—a Jewish religious party that flourished during the last two centuries before Christ and during the first Christian century. Jesus criticized them for their lack of compassion, for their failure to practice what they preached, and for their contempt for people who could not obey the law as carefully as the Pharisees did. (Mercer)

Sherry didn't sleep with her boyfriend for fear of what her mother would say if she found out. One day Sherry slept with her boyfriend, and as she feared, her mother found out. Sherry lost her motivation to obey, so she began sleeping with him regularly. Obeying God because of others' opinions might work for a while, but it won't honor God. Eventually, it won't work at all.

You may control your anger because your father scolded you severely when you lost your temper. But in reflecting on the proper motivations for obedience, you can choose to replace that motivation with an understanding that losing your temper dishonors God. Self-control and a proper expression of displeasure bring honor to Him.

Think about a time when you did the right thing for the wrong reason—for fear of what others would think. What lesson(s) did you learn from this experience?

_____

_____

2. God Will Be Angry with Me

Hank was afraid that God would zap him if he did anything wrong, so he performed many good deeds for God. He lived each day in fear of God's anger. Predictably, his relationship with the Lord was cold and mechanical.

We've already discussed the difference between God's discipline and punishment. We know God disciplines us in love, not in anger. His response to our sin is grief, not condemnation.

God doesn't want us to fear His anger but to respond to His love. This produces joyful obedience instead of fear. He genuinely is concerned for your welfare. Realizing that He loves you and wants the best for you can prompt you to obey in response to His love. It will motivate you to honor the One who loves you.

We know God disciplines us in love, not in anger.

3. I Couldn't Approve of Myself If I Didn't Obey

Some people obey God in an effort to live up to certain standards they've set for themselves. Sadly, the idea of yielding their lives to a loving Lord often is far from their minds. If they don't meet those standards, they feel ashamed.

These people primarily are concerned with do's and don'ts. Instead of having an intimate relationship with God, they see the

Christian life as a ritual, with the key emphasis on rules. They tend to compare themselves with others, hoping to be accepted on the basis of being a little better than someone else.

God gave us His commands out of love for us. As we obey Him, we are protected and freed to enjoy life more fully.

4. I'll Obey to Be Blessed

If our sole motive to obey is to receive God's blessing or special favor, we simply are attempting to manipulate God. The underlying assumption is: I've been good enough … bless me. It's true that we will reap what we sow. It's true that obedience keeps us within God's plan for our lives. But our decision to obey never should be based solely on God's rewarding us.

Have you ever found yourself trying to make a deal with God or trying to manipulate God for your own good? In the margin write one example.

One reason you might try to make a deal with God is your high view of yourself. Perhaps you see yourself as someone who deserves the best from Him. But we are not His equals. He is the awesome, almighty Creator; we are sinful people, deserving eternal condemnation. By His grace He forgives and accepts us.

After learning about these four motivations, think about your own life. Do you have poor reasons for obeying God? Check the statement(s) that apply to you.

- ❏ God will be angry with me if I don't.
- ❏ I obey to be blessed.
- ❏ Someone may find out.
- ❏ I couldn't approve of myself if I didn't obey.
- ❏ Christ's love motivates me to live for Him.
- ❏ Other: _____

Changing the Way You Do Things

If you want to change your self-serving motivations to motivations that will honor God, several ways exist to get you started.
- As you read the Bible, look for characteristics of God
- Thank God for His discipline, realizing that it protects us from the destructive nature of sin.
- Ask the Holy Spirit to help you uphold God's commands, knowing that He gives them for our spiritual growth.
- Focus not just on the here and now but keep your sights on eternity.

Week 4
The Performance Trap

"I must meet certain standards to feel good about myself."

DON'S BATTLE WITH FEAR

It was Don's senior year of high school, and he was in the state track meet finals. Don was not supposed to be in the finals, but there he was. What a great opportunity! Close to the finish line, Don was near the front runners. All of a sudden he came up lame.

Now, many years later, Don is not sure whether he really was injured or whether he used the pain as an excuse for not trying at the very end of the race. He questions whether he gave away an opportunity to be successful for fear of trying and then failing.

A key verse to memorize this week:

Surely you desire truth in the inner parts;
you teach me wisdom in the inmost place.
Psalm 51:6, NIV

In week 2 we considered the negative consequences of the performance trap—one of Satan's many lies. In week 3 we drew comfort from God's plan to justify us through His Son's death on the cross when we repent of our sins. Then, Christ's righteousness becomes our own in God's sight. We are freely forgiven.

This week we are digging deeper into the process for healing from the performance trap—learning to reach possible standards by appropriate efforts. Fortunately, God's truth is reliable. You can count on it!

The Plight of the Perfectionist

Let's begin by asking some questions.
1. Why do we sometimes tolerate failure in another person but cannot tolerate it in ourselves?
2. If we cannot tolerate failure, how many of life's opportunities will we allow to pass us by without our taking the challenge?
3. How different would your life be if it were not for the performance trap?

Most of us are unaware of how thoroughly Satan has deceived us. He has led us blindly down a path of destruction, making us captives of our inability to meet our standards consistently. We are in danger of becoming hopelessly self-centered. Satan has shackled us in chains that keep us from experiencing the love, freedom, and purposes of Christ.

> Be careful that no one takes you captive through philosophy and empty deceit based on human tradition, based on the elemental forces of the world, and not based on Christ.
>
> Colossians 2:8

In Colossians 2:8 Paul warns us of the power to become a captive or slave of the wrong things. Read the verse in the margin. Underline the basis for our Christian philosophy of life.

Indeed, we've reached a true mark of maturity when we begin testing the deceitful thoughts of our minds against the Word of God. We no longer have to live by our fleshly thoughts; we have the mind of Christ (1 Corinthians 2:16). Through His Spirit, we can challenge the indoctrinations and traditions that have long held us in guilt and condemnation. We can then replace those deceptions with the powerful truth of the Scriptures.

The Lure of Success

A primary deception all of us tend to believe is that success will bring fulfillment and happiness. We've tried to measure up, thinking that if we could meet certain standards, we would feel good about ourselves. But again and again, we've failed and have felt miserable. Even if we succeed on a fairly regular basis, occasional failure may be so devastating that it dominates our perception of ourselves.

Think of a time when you were successful in a task or project. Circle the feelings that were true of you then.

Elated	Surprised	Exhausted	Disappointed
Energized	Proud	Disillusioned	Happy

Did you feel great for a while, or did the success provide even more pressure to do better in the future? Failure to meet certain standards threatens our security and self-confidence. Our attitudes and behavior reflect Satan's distortion of the truth. Because of our unique personalities, we each react very differently to this deception. Some of us respond by becoming slaves to perfection, constantly driving ourselves toward attaining goals.

Some of us become slaves to perfection.

Because they are usually more competent than most, perfectionists see nothing wrong with their compulsive behavior. "I just like to see things well done," a perfectionist may say. There's nothing wrong with doing things well. The problem is that perfectionists usually base their self-worth on their ability to accomplish a goal. Therefore, failure is a threat and unacceptable to them.

Reread the story of Don in the introduction to this week's study (p. 53). In your own words, why did Don give away his chance at a medal?

_____

Recall the effects of the performance trap from week 2 (pp. 25–31). The more you can objectively evaluate your tendency toward perfectionism, the more likely you will understand why you believe and act a certain way. List the tendencies of the performance trap that pose more of a problem for you.

_____

Jane's mother had criticized her all of her life. Every day Jane got a full report on what she had done wrong. Jane tried to please her mother. Every day she made a list of things she could accomplish. She checked off the things that got done and felt guilty about the things left undone. No matter how much Jane did, her mother was never pleased. Jane believed that if she tried harder, made even better choices, did more than she was asked to do around the house, she could eventually win her mother's approval.

What do you think will eventually happen to Jane?

_____

We have four false beliefs firmly fixed in our minds because of all the things we have experienced in life. In this week's Scripture, Psalm 51:6, we are reminded to look to God for wisdom in our innermost selves—those parts of us that are most vulnerable. Begin memorizing this verse now.

Day 2
Testing Our Thoughts

Without the Holy Spirit's guidance, we all have difficulty being real. In spite of our best efforts, it usually takes only one perceived failure for despair to set in. Our worst fears have come to pass. Instead of thinking, *I failed,* we pronounce ourselves failures. Despair means seeing no hope. Even with the honesty, love, and encouragement of at least one other person, we easily become depressed because of the extent of our wounds.

Read the following Scriptures, and after each one write the truth of God's Word that you find there.

"There is therefore now no condemnation for those who are in Christ Jesus" (Romans 8:1).

_____

"Who will separate us from the love of Christ? Will tribulation, or distress, or persecution, or famine, or nakedness, or peril, or sword?" (Romans 8:35).

_____

"It was for freedom that Christ set us free; therefore keep standing firm and do not be subject again to a yoke of slavery" (Galatians 5:1).

_____

"He has now reconciled you in His fleshly body through death, in order to present you before Him holy and blameless and beyond reproach" (Colossians 1:22).

_____

"I am writing to you, little children, because your sins have been forgiven you for His name's sake" (1 John 2:12).

_____

How We React to Satan's Deception

Many of us respond by becoming slaves to perfectionism. We drive ourselves over and over toward reaching goals. We accept the false belief: I must meet certain standards in order to feel good about myself. When we believe this lie about ourselves, our attitudes and behavior reflect Satan's distortion of truth.

Most of us exhibit some combination of perfectionism and withdrawal. We are willing to take risks and to work hard in the areas in which we feel sure of success, but we avoid the people and situations that may bring rejection and failure.

Check the box beside the words or phrases below that characterize a person exhibiting withdrawal.

- ❏ Avoidance
- ❏ Risk taker
- ❏ Fears disapproval
- ❏ Fears rejection

- ❏ Willing to be vulnerable
- ❏ Avoids demanding relationships
- ❏ Volunteers
- ❏ Runs from situations that may not be successful

Others of us go into a tailspin of despair. When we base our security on success and on others' opinions, we become dependent on our abilities to perform and to please others. We develop a have-to mentality: I have to do well on this exam (or my security as a good student will be threatened). I have to make that deal (or it will mean my boss will think I am a failure). My father (or mother, spouse, friend) has to be happy with my decisions (because I cannot cope with his/her disapproval). God does not leave us in this misery. He helps us know ourselves and know God's truth.

Read 2 Timothy 3:16-17 in the margin. Describe in your own words how the Scriptures can help you.

_____

_____

All Scripture is inspired by God and profitable for teaching, for reproof, for correction, for training in righteousness; so that the man of God may be adequate, equipped for every good work.

2 Timothy 3:16-17

Looking at Why We Do Christian Activities

Some people try to obtain a more positive sense of self-worth through activities they perform as an outgrowth of being Christians. They may be doing what they believe the Bible instructs them to do, but they may be doing the proverbial right thing for the wrong reason. They may be seeking recognition and approval, and they continue with them to avoid the fear of failure.

List below some activities you perform as an outgrowth of being a Christian. Ask God to show you if any of these you do to increase your self-worth, rather than feeling led by the Spirit to do them.

1. _____ 3. _____

2. _____ 4. _____

Have you entered some relationships with selfish personal goals, which could cause you to manipulate others in an effort to reach those goals? Sometimes we even use kind and encouraging remarks to get others to do what we want them to do. Sooner or later, they usually realize that we are actually manipulating them. They may become bitter and stay away from us.

In turn, if people prevent us from meeting our standards, we might become angry, enraged, or resentful; we might blame them, reject them, or withdraw from them. We think they have kept us from meeting one of our deepest needs!

Read Matthew 6:5-6 . What did Jesus say about people who perform religious acts just to get attention or approval?

_____

Unwillingness to Share Our Faith
Perhaps the most critical result of the fear of rejection keeps many of us from sharing our faith. Nonbelievers are well aware of the pain of rejection, and they use it to threaten us so they won't have to deal with the gospel. Their rejection quickly sends the message, "I don't care about you or what you have to say." So, since we fear rejection anyway, we quickly back off. Some things they say are:

- "You don't believe all that Christianity junk, do you?"
- "How could anyone with any brains be a Christian?"
- "Christianity is a crutch."
- "I believe religion is a personal issue. Don't talk to me about it."
- "Only losers are Christians."

Has someone used a put-down remark to prevent you from sharing the gospel? If so, what did they say?

_____

When you pray, you are not to be like the hypocrites; for they love to stand and pray in the synagogues and on the street corners so that they may be seen by men. Truly I say to you, they have their reward in full. But you, when you pray, go into your inner room, close your door and pray to your Father who is in secret, and your Father who sees what is done in secret will reward you.

Matthew 6:5-6

What are nonbelievers doing? They are rejecting us (inflicting emotional pain) to silence us. Identifying this fear and working through it may enable us to more readily initiate conversation with others about the gospel.

The issue is more than just doing the right things. Are you doing the right things for the right reasons? Jesus had the most trouble with religious people who were doing religious works for the wrong reasons.

If you are honest, you probably perform some of your good deeds to make yourself more acceptable to others, to God, and perhaps to yourself. The focus of our lives should be on Christ, not on ourselves; nor should the focus be self-imposed regulations.

The lordship of Christ is dependent on our moment-by-moment attention to His direction. Even doing Christian activities, we may feel that if we do these we'll be more successful as a person. Even Christian standards of perfection, if used to obtain self-worth apart from God's plan, go against God's truth.

Read Romans 8:28 in the margin. In your own words write the way God wants to use things that happen in your life.

> We know that all things work together for the good of those who love God: those who are called according to His purpose.
>
> Romans 8:28

_____

As you become less influenced by the fear of failure, you can be happier, more loving, and more thankful to God for His love.

Day 3
Getting Our Attention

As long as we operate according to Satan's lies, we will likely fear failure. We must realize that as Christians, we have the Holy Spirit's power provided to lay aside deceptive ways of thinking and to renew our minds by the truth of God's Word.

For our benefit God often allows us to experience circumstances that will enable us to see how blindly we stick to Satan's deceptions. Many times these circumstances seem very negative, but through them we can learn valuable, life-changing truths.

In Psalm 107:35-36 we see a poetic example of this process:

> He changes a wilderness into a pool of water
> And a dry land into springs of water;
> And there He makes the hungry to dwell,
> So that they may establish an inhabited city.

Has your fruitful land become a salt waste? Maybe God is trying to get your attention to teach you a tremendously important lesson—that success or failure is not the basis of your self-worth. Maybe the only way you can learn this lesson is by experiencing the pain of failure. In His great love God leads us through experiences that are difficult but important to our growth.

List below some ways you think God might be trying to get your attention on this matter.

What a Way to Learn

The more sensitive you become to the fear of failure and the problems it may cause, the more you can understand your own behavior as well as that of others. The fear of failure is like stacking marbles—a difficult task but not any more difficult than trying to win the performance game. When we evaluate ourselves by our performance, we're ultimately going to lose, no matter how successful we are at the moment.

A rat placed in a box and shocked until it huddles in one particular corner soon learns to run to that corner as soon as it is placed in the box. Even though God means for us to experience the freedom of His love and eternal purpose, how much time do we spend huddled in a corner like a laboratory rat? How much of our energy do we expend in order to avoid the disapproving "shocks" of those around us?

The focus of the gospel is on relationships, not regulations.

The focus of the gospel is on relationships, not regulations. Christ's exercise of His lordship in our lives depends on our listening to His moment-by-moment instruction. Looking only at rules will keep us in a mental prison because we always have to examine ourselves.

On the other hand, we may feel very good about ourselves because we are winning the performance game. We may be so talented that we are reaching virtually every goal we have set for ourselves. We can't afford to mistake pride for positive self-worth. Pride is a sin. Realize that God is able to bring about whatever circumstances are necessary to defeat pride and cause us to stop trusting in ourselves. God intends to bring us to Himself through prayer and the study of His Word so that we can know, love, and serve Him. Sometimes He allows us to fail miserably so we will look to Him instead of to ourselves for positive self-worth. Our security and significance only come from above.

Sometimes He allows us to fail miserably.

Day 4
The Process of Hope and Healing

To grow and become the person Christ intends for us, several factors must be present. These factors are not steps we can accomplish one right after the other. They are ingredients that promote growth when they all work at the same time and over a period of time. These factors include:

- Honesty
- Affirming relationships
- Right thinking
- The Holy Spirit
- Time

If any of these is missing in a person's life, then his or her progress will be slowed down, if not stopped completely.

Is one of the factors listed above missing in your life? Circle:

Yes   No   Why?_____

Which do you see working most strongly in your life?

_____

Let's examine these five ingredients.

Honesty
We can experience healing only to the degree that we are aware we need it. If we are completely unaware of our dishonesty, we won't seek a solution. If we have only a dim awareness of our

dishonesty, we may seek (and find) remedies that only scratch the surface of our need.

But if someone encourages us to be honest at a deeper level about our painful needs, then we can experience the power of healing and comfort at that particular level.

Surely you desire truth in the inner parts; you teach me wisdom in the inmost place.
Psalm 51:6, NIV

Read Psalm 51:6, our memory verse. From this passage and the above paragraph, why do you think the Lord wants us to be honest with Him, with others, and with ourselves?

❏ Honesty is the best policy.
❏ The Bible tells us not to lie to one another.
❏ Honesty is the first crucial step toward real change.
❏ Other?_____

Honesty helps us go beyond a surface awareness of our need to deal with healing at a deeper level. The Lord wants us to be honest with ourselves, with Him, and with at least one other person. We need honesty in our lives because it is the first important step toward healing and maturity and helps us go beyond surface awareness.

Check the statement you feel best describes how honest you are about your needs.

❏ I am completely honest and objective about myself all the time.
❏ Most of the time I am honest and objective about myself.
❏ Seldom am I honest or objective about myself.
❏ Never am I honest or objective about myself.

If none of the people around us tell us otherwise, we may believe we are completely honest about ourselves. We think we're objective—able to look at ourselves with an open mind.

Those of us from relatively stable backgrounds usually find it easier to be honest about the joys and pain in our lives. Some of us, however, come from dysfunctional families and have experienced tragedies that have caused deep wounds. These experiences prompt us to put up defenses designed to block pain.

Defensive barriers often keep us from seeing problem areas in our lives. To those who sincerely ask, God gives increased understanding in order to determine what parts of our lives need change or adjustment.

Affirming Relationships

Without some affirmation from others, people seldom have the courage to be honest about their lives. The love, strength, and honesty we find in other people truly are Godlike traits.

A friend, a small group, a pastor, or a counselor who won't be frustrated by our slow progress—and who won't give us quick and easy solutions—is a valuable find! This person can listen to us instead of lecturing us. This friend will not jump to making judgmental statements about what we say.

Of course, we must use good judgment about what and with whom we share. Pray that God will provide a person or group of persons with whom you can be open and honest, who objectively can listen to you and share with you, and who will encourage you to make real, rather than surface, progress. This type of person truly is a treasure!

We must use good judgment about what and with whom we share.

If you are not reading this as part of a small group study, consider the benefits of a group setting. Not only can you gain positive skills as the group progresses, but you can have the valuable experience of learning from other group members.

In the margin write the names of people who have affirmed or encouraged you (see p. 11).

Check the statement(s) that best expresses how these persons' affirmation affected you.

- ❏ I gained a sense of confidence.
- ❏ I felt encouraged.
- ❏ I withdrew from the person.
- ❏ I did not feel I deserved the affirmation.
- ❏ I felt that this person was not being honest about me.
- ❏ I thanked God for sending such a person my way.

When you named persons who had affirmed you, one of your children may be among your major supporters. Perhaps you named a neighbor. You could have named someone you see often or only occasionally. I hope someone—your parents, a friend, a teacher, your spouse, or a group—is quick to say that he/she loves and values you. You can be such a friend to others.

Check the statement(s) on page 64 that best describes the effect this person (or group) has on you.

❏ This person or group listens to me.

❏ This person or group encourages my honesty.

❏ This person or group accepts my strengths and weaknesses.

❏ This person or group gives me respect and support.

❏ This person or group prays for me regularly.

If you have not yet found someone who will encourage and affirm you, stop now and pray for God's leadership in this decision. You may want to consider someone in your group. Generally, when we affirm others, they affirm us.

Day 5
More of the Process

Many of us don't know what we really believe about God and about ourselves. We often say what we don't mean and mean what we don't say. God's Word is our guide for truth. It is truly "a lamp to our feet and a light to our path" (Psalm 119:105). Yet we often have trouble applying the Scripture to our lives because over the years we have structured so many elaborate defenses to protect ourselves.

We must realize that God speaks to us through Scripture to identify and attack these defensive barriers. We can experience an open and honest relationship with God. Growth includes understanding more about God's love, forgiveness, and power.

As God speaks to us through the Scripture, we learn about life, where our views are in error, and how to correct our faulty perceptions so that we continually experience the process of growth. This verse from Hebrews describes just how powerful Scripture can be in our lives.

> The word of God is living and active and sharper than any two-edged sword, and piercing as far as the division of soul and spirit, of both joints and marrow, and able to judge the thoughts and intentions of the heart. And there is no creature hidden from His sight, but all things are open and laid bare to the eyes of Him with whom we have to do.
>
> Hebrews 4:12-13

Think of how you have developed your thoughts and beliefs. In the list rank each item from 1 to 8 to indicate what effect it had on forming your thoughts and beliefs.

_____ Books	_____ Television programs
_____ Movies	_____ Friends
_____ Family	_____ God
_____ Neighbors	_____ Church

All of the above have influenced our lives and deeply affected our thoughts and beliefs. All of them together have made you a unique individual. What part does the Holy Spirit play in helping to shape our thinking?

The Holy Spirit Helps Us Grow

Deep spiritual growth requires giving attention to the whole person—emotional, relational, physical, and spiritual. God gives us the Holy Spirit to communicate His love, light, forgiveness, and power. These qualities minister to our deepest needs. This spiritual aspect of healing is the most basic aspect of growth because our view of God (and our relationship with Him) determine the quality and degree of health we experience in every area of our lives.

Some of us believe that only positive, pleasant emotions like love and joy characterize the Holy Spirit's ministry. However, the Holy Spirit produces honesty and courage in our lives as we grapple with the reality of pain. This is one of the miracles of the Holy Spirit's work! He is the Spirit of truth, not of denial. He enables us to experience each element of spiritual growth as He gives us wisdom, strength, and encouragement through God's Word and through other people.

The Holy Spirit is the source of spiritual wisdom, insight, and power. He uses the Word of God and the people of God to instruct us and to model for us the character of Christ.

Read John 14:16-17 in the margin. How do you feel when you realize that the Holy Spirit is the Spirit of truth in your life? Circle all that apply or write your own.

Exposed	Grateful	Hopeful	Secure
Uncomfortable	Scared	Amazed	Wary

_____

I will ask the Father, and He will give you another Counselor to be with you forever. He is the Spirit of truth, whom the world is unable to receive because it doesn't see Him or know Him. But you do know Him, because He remains with you and will be in you.

John 14:16-17, HCSB

Give Growth Time to Bring Fruit

Don't we sometimes wish we were computers so that solutions to our problems would occur in microseconds? People, however, don't change that quickly.

In the Scripture we see many references to agriculture. The Scripture depicts seasons of planting, weeding, watering, growing, and harvesting. Farmers don't expect to plant seeds in the morning and harvest their crops that afternoon. Seeds must go through a complete cycle of growth before they mature. They receive plenty of attention in the process.

In this age of instant coffee, microwave dinners, and electronic banking, we assume that spiritual, emotional, and relational health will be rapid also. These unrealistic expectations only cause discouragement and disappointment.

Our growth will be stunted and superficial if we don't emphasize properly the essential five elements: honesty about our emotions, affirming relationships, right thinking promoted through Bible study and applying the Bible to our lives, the ministry of the Holy Spirit, and time.

We can remember that all of these elements are required to produce growth and health.

Check the sentences below that best express the reasons we tend to get impatient and to expect fast results.

❏ We don't want to experience hurt.
❏ Others say something like a seminar or a book helped them instantly.
❏ Technological advances in society encourage us to expect dramatic results at the push of a button.
❏ When we experience a spurt of insight and healing, we conclude that the rest of the process should be quick and easy.

Our growth toward wholeness and maturity is a journey which we can't complete fully until we join the Lord in heaven. The apostle Paul understood this truth and saw himself as being in the middle of this process. He wrote about this to the believers at Philippi.

Read Philippians 3:12-14. Then indicate whether the following statements are T (true) or F (false).

_____ Paul felt he already had obtained his goal.
_____ Paul felt he was not perfect.
_____ Paul was in the process of obtaining his goal.
_____ Paul forgot the past and was looking to the future.

... not that I have already reached the goal or am already fully mature, but I make every effort to take hold of it because I also have been taken hold of by Christ Jesus. Brothers, I do not consider myself to have taken hold of it. But one thing I do: forgetting what is behind and reaching forward to what is ahead, I pursue as my goal the prize promised by God's heavenly call in Christ Jesus.

Philippians 3:12-14

If Paul, the foremost missionary and writer of much of the New Testament, saw himself as being "in the process," we can feel encouraged to continue in the process toward change as well. All statements but the first are true.

Review

Consider this: Who do you talk to the most? Yourself, of course. What do you talk to yourself about the most? Yourself, of course. What is the main topic of the conversation you are having with yourself about yourself? Much of the time you think about how well you're doing based on your performance and others' opinions of you. How many times in your life have you used the formula:

Self-Worth = Performance + Others' Opinions

When you equate your self-worth with performance and others' opinions, you are judging yourself based on a satanic formula designed to enslave you in the performance trap. Thankfully, God has canceled this equation altogether! He has given us a secure self-worth totally apart from our ability to perform. We have been justified and placed in right standing before God through Christ's death on the cross, which paid for our sins. But God didn't stop with our forgiveness; He also granted us the very righteousness of Christ (2 Corinthians 5:21)!

Complete the statement of God's truth that demolishes Satan's first lie: I must meet certain standards to feel good about myself (see p. 128).

Because of _____

_____

I no longer_____

Week 5
Approval Addict

I must have the approval of others to feel good about myself.

MOTIVATED TO SERVE?

Helen loved to be needed by other people. If a friend had a problem, Helen was right there to listen and comfort. She often volunteered her help, even when no one asked for it. Everyone knew they could count on good old Helen to come through for them.

Helen expected that her kind words and deeds would bring her praise and friendships. But now, Helen felt exhausted. Instead of having her emotional needs met, she began to feel used and abused by others. Was Helen a sacrificial saint? Were her deeds Christ-driven or self-driven? What do you think will happen to Helen?

A key verse to memorize this week:

Am I now seeking the favor of men, or of God? Or am I striving to please men? If I were still trying to please men, I would not be a bondservant of Christ.

Galatians 1:10

Words to help you understand this week's lessons:

reconciliation (n.)—to restore to friendship or harmony; to settle or resolve something. *(Example: You are acceptable to God because of **reconciliation**.)*

mercy (n.)—God's attitude toward people in distress; compassion for the ills of others. *(Example: God saved us according to His **mercy**.)*

Though God does not intend it, our self-worth is largely determined by what others think. As a result, the need for their approval can drive us to do whatever we feel we must do to receive it. This week we'll uncover the blessings of getting our approval from God. This week's Scripture clearly teaches that we can't be a servant of Christ if we are "still trying to please men."

Day 1

Becoming Friends

Helen is typical of many of us. The false belief associated with Helen's behavior is that we must have approval of certain others to feel good about ourselves. This is the second of Satan's lies.

As we learned in week 2, we spend much of our time building relationships and striving to win others' respect. Sometimes we give of ourselves to the point of exhaustion because we feel that doing so will make people appreciate us and will keep them from rejecting us.

Fortunately, God has solution for those who seek approval in the wrong places. It's called reconciliation. By becoming friends of God, He will meet our need for approval. Let's see how this transformation takes place.

No longer do I call you slaves, for the slave does not know what his master is doing; but I have called you friends, for all things that I have heard from My Father I have made known to you.

John 15:15

To recap, write below the second false belief and the emotions that arise from it. Then write God's truth (p. 128).

2. I must have _____

_____ .

(the fear of _____)

Because of _____

_____

_____

How Others' Expectations Affect Me

When we admit to people-pleasing behavior, we can begin to identify the negative results and to know how to change them. The example below demonstrates what someone might write if she feels rejection or disapproval from her father.

Example:
1. My father would be more pleased with me if I called him more often, wore my hair the way he wants me to, and got a better-paying job.

2. My father is proud of me when I get a promotion, remember important family dates, and win in sports.
3. My father criticizes me, speaks sarcastically, and sometimes ignores me in an effort to get me to change.
4. To gain my father's approval, I tell him only what he likes to hear, exaggerate the truth a little, and work really hard to be a success.

Now you fill in the blanks, based on your experience.

1. _____ would be more pleased with me

if I would— _____

2. _____ is proud of me when I— _____

_____

3. _____ attempts to get me to change by—

_____

_____

4. Things I do or say to get _____ to approve of

me include— _____

_____

An Approval Addict's Confession

I easily can identify with people who find themselves hungry for others' approval. My own desire for this has often been so great that I joke about having been born an approval addict. As I grew up, I always felt that I didn't fit in—I was different from others, Something was inherently wrong with me. I desperately hoped that winning others' favor would make up for the negative feelings I had about myself.

Ironically, others' conditional approval never was enough to satisfy me. Instead, being praised only reminded me of the disapproval I might encounter if I failed to maintain what I had achieved. Thus I was driven to work even harder at being success-ful. I occasionally find myself falling into this pattern of behavior again, despite what I know and have experienced. Through my relationship with God and His truth, here's what I've learned:

The only way we can overcome the fear of rejection is to focus on the reality of God's acceptance of us based on our position in Christ. Otherwise, we are left to focus on others' approval based on our performance.

Our fear of rejection will control us to the degree to which we base our worth on the opinions of others rather than on our relationship with God. Depending on others for value brings slavery, while abiding in Christ's love and acceptance brings freedom and joy.

Our emotional responses to others may vary from slight annoyance to deep hurt, anger, and bitterness. We fear rejection to the degree that we base our self-worth on the opinions of others. If we believe the lie, *I am what others say I am,* the fear of rejection will plague us.

In Galatians 1:10 Paul clearly drew the line concerning our search for approval. We ultimately seek either people's approval or God's approval as the basis of our self-worth. We cannot seek both. God wants to be the Lord of our lives. He is unwilling to share that rightful lordship with anyone else.

> Am I now seeking the favor of men, or of God? Or am I striving to please men? If I were still trying to please men, I would not be a bond-servant of Christ.
>
> Galatians 1:10

Here's a thought to remember: Only God, speaking to us through His Word, His Spirit, and His timing, can provide the security we so desperately seek.

What Will You Do?

What will you do to be a more accepting person? More willing to forgive? Basing your self-worth on God's Word? Will you claim your importance to Him? Will you commit to remembering that you need not fear rejection because God loves you? If so, allow God to lead you to another person who needs acceptance. Be God's instrument of peace in his or her life.

Day 2

Acceptable and Accepting

Feeling Unacceptable

Edith was an unmarried woman who gave birth to a child. Although she was a Christian before this event occurred, Edith later stopped attending church because she no longer felt close to God. Although she believed God forgives some sins, she felt that her action was on God's unpardonable list. She spent much of her adult life feeling unworthy of God's love. Edith is like many of us. We look back on our lives and think about something we've done that seems so horrible, so inexcusable, so terribly wrong that we don't think we'll ever feel acceptable again. We think, *I deserve to be rejected because of this big mess.*

Think of a past event about which you still have a tinge of guilt. In fact, you may be wondering how you can be acceptable in God's eyes because of it. Ask God to show you His forgiveness as you continue to read this week.

God's solution to the sin dilemma is **reconciliation.** Because Christ has reconciled us to God, He has wiped our slate clean. He has no reason hold on to some sin.

Recall the definition of *reconciliation* from page 68. In your own words, write what the term means to you.

_____

_____

God's solution to the fear of rejection is based on Christ's sacrificial payment for our sins. Through Christ's payment, we find forgiveness, reconciliation, and total acceptance.

In Colossians 1:21-22 Paul describes how we go from a relationship of being enemies to being friends with God. Below is my summary of that passage.

> Because of your sin you were an enemy of God and were hostile in mind. Your sin made you subject to God's wrath; but if you have trusted Christ, you now are declared holy in His sight, without blemish and free from accusation. (author's translation)

Not Simply a Ticket to Heaven

The fact that Christ accepts us unconditionally is a profound, life-changing truth.

The fact that Christ accepts us unconditionally is a profound, life-changing truth. Salvation is not simply a ticket to heaven. It is the beginning of a dynamic new relationship with God. *Justification,* which we defined in week 4, explains the judicial facts of our forgiveness and righteousness in Christ. *Reconciliation* explains the relational aspect. The moment we receive Christ by faith, we enter a personal relationship with Him.

Recently, in a group prayer meeting someone prayed, "Thank You, God, for accepting me when I am so unacceptable."

Read Romans 5:8-11 in your Bible. What is wrong with the statement you just read: "Thank You, God, for accepting me when I am so unacceptable"?

_____

This person understood that we cannot earn God's acceptance by our own merit. However, this person seems to have forgotten that we are accepted unconditionally in Christ. Through claiming Christ's death and resurrection as payment for our sins, we have become acceptable to God. He does not just tolerate us. This bond did not occur because God decided He could overlook our sin but because Christ chose to present us to the Father holy and blameless.

Mark the following statements as T (true) or F (false).

_____ I am acceptable to God right now.
_____ I go back and forth. Some days I'm acceptable; others, I'm not.
_____ I am 99.99 percept acceptable to God.
_____ I am acceptable because I do good deeds.
_____ I am acceptable because Christ has paid the price.

You are one hundred percent acceptable to the highest Judge: the perfect, holy, and righteous God Almighty. You are acceptable to God for one reason: Christ abolished the barrier and made peace with God through His blood on the cross. You have the righteousness of Christ (2 Corinthians 5:21). You can never be any more acceptable to God than you are now (Romans 5:8-10; Ephesians 2:14-18).

You fear rejection when you believe the lie, _I am what others think of me_ instead of believing God's truth, _I am totally acceptable and accepted because of Christ._ You will begin to experience freedom from the fear of rejection when you believe God has completely accepted you. If you refuse to believe, the only other option is turning to others, which will leave you painfully disillusioned.

Turning to others will leave you painfully disillusioned.

We Do Our Share of Rejecting, Too

Before we can be sure we're on the right track toward overcoming our fear of rejection, we must look at how we treat people. Do we communicate rejection to others? Have you ever been guilty of using disapproval, silence, sarcasm, or criticism to get others to do what you want them to do?

In the margin write a remark you think others would consider a rejection.

Four Basic Levels of Acceptance and Rejection

Perhaps you consider yourself a very accepting person. The four basic levels of rejection and acceptance center on the question, What does a person have to do to be accepted by you? Here are examples of what each level communicates.

1. **Total rejection:** "No matter what you do, it's not good enough."
2. **Highly conditional acceptance:** "You must do these things in order for me to be happy with you."
3. **Mildly conditional acceptance:** "I will be happier with you if you do these things."
4. **Unconditional acceptance:** "There is nothing you can do that can make me stop loving/befriending you."

You may find yourself wondering, *How, then, do I relate to persons who manipulate me? How do I relate to persons who I fear will reject me? How do I relate to persons whose approval I feel I so desperately need?* The answer is this: We relate to them in the way God relates to us. We can do nothing to make Him stop loving us or to love us more. He accepts us as we are. He loves us unconditionally.

Unconditional acceptance truly is the biblical way to relate to others. This does not mean that we can do as we please or that we are to ignore unacceptable behavior in others. Unconditional acceptance may include loving confrontation; correction; and, in some cases, discipline. We must learn to separate the person from his or her behavior. We accept this person as loved by God and as important to Him as we think we may be.

We must turn this person loose from the power he or she holds over us. We do not need this person's approval for our self-worth. We have God's approval, and that's all that matters. However, we may choose to look to other encouragers for friendship.

The Biblical Theme of Reconciliation

No greater theme exists in Scripture than the reconciliation of people to God. Study the passages and answer the question after each one.

Psalm 103:12. What happens to our transgressions (sins)?

_____

Matthew 26:28. Why was Christ's blood shed? _____

_____

John 3:16. What is God's promise? _____

_____

Day 3
A New Way to React

Paul said, "He saved us, not on the basis of deeds which we have done in righteousness, but according to His **mercy**" (Titus 3:5). Christ has reconciled us to God and allows us to experience the incredible truth, *We are totally accepted by and acceptable to God.*

This statement doesn't mean that we won't feel pain or anger when things don't go our way. We need to be honest about our feelings. Covering them up doesn't help. However, if we quickly seek God's perspective on whatever we are experiencing, we can apply this truth in every difficult situation—whether that situation involves someone's disapproval, our own failure to accomplish something, or the failure of another person.

Here's an example:
- **Situation:** Frank laughed at my idea in the committee meeting. (Others laughed too.)
- **Feelings:** I felt deeply hurt and didn't say another word. I left as soon as the meeting was over.
- **Emotions:** Hurt, anger, rejection, and fear.
- **New response:** I do not need Frank's acceptance (nor that of the other committee members). I can feel good about myself, because I am deeply loved, completely forgiven, fully pleasing, totally accepted, and absolutely complete in Jesus Christ.

Do you recall having read the last statement before? It is part of "My Identity in Christ" (p.113). If you have not memorized it, do so now. You can use these same words with any situation in your life when you have experienced rejection and that rejection has

We need to be honest about our feelings. Covering them up doesn't help.

75

caused you pain or hurt. After you have used this self-talk several times, it will start to become a habit.

The Biblical Theme of Reconciliation

Continue your study on the theme of reconciliation by reading the following Scriptures and answering these questions:

Romans 8:33. Who will accuse us? _____

_____

Romans 8:38-39. What can separate us from God's love?

_____

2 Corinthians 5:17. Describe what we are in Christ.

_____

Because of reconciliation we enjoy a full and complete relationship with Christ. In this relationship He does not determine our value based on others' approval. However, we may question what this relationship means as we attempt to apply it in our day-to-day experience. Let's analyze this issue.

Hard to Change Our Outlook

When we are born again as spiritual infants in right standing with God, we are still tilted toward the world's way of thinking. Because the world's outlook and values have conditioned us, we find it hard to look at things God's way.

Indeed, when Paul wrote to the Christians at Corinth, he called them men of flesh. Though they were Christians, these individuals had not yet developed into the complete, mature believers God intended them to be. In another letter, Paul referred to believers as babes in Christ.

Many of us are like the Christians at Corinth. We still try to get our significance the world's way—through success and approval. Sometimes we do this even through our church activities.

For five years in a row, Janet had organized the churchwide picnic. She was well known for her lavish decorations and her efficiency at putting committees to work. Then one year the youth in the

Because the world's outlook and values have conditioned us, we find it hard to look at things God's way.

church asked if they could be in charge of the picnic so they could learn leadership skills. When the youth asked her for assistance, Janet became so angry that she refused to cooperate. Janet and her family eventually began attending another church because Janet felt her entire self-worth was based on her history as the organizer of the church picnic.

Think for a moment. Have you ever acted like Janet and felt your self-worth was lessened when you lost a role you held in a church or another organization? If so, describe what happened and how you handled the situation.

_____

_____

The desire for success and approval may become the basis of an addictive lifestyle. As we begin to base our self-worth on God's approval, we may feel some pain of withdrawal, but we will begin to discover true freedom and maturity in Christ. We will understand that our lives mean much more than worldly success or the approval others can bring.

Write below the second truth from God's Word to refute Satan's second lie (see p. 128).

Truth: _____

_____

Day 4
Healthy Relationships

Parents as Models

God intends for parents to model His character to their children. Scripture says parents are to give their children affection, compassion, protection, provision, and loving discipline. When parents provide this kind of environment in their home, children usually can understand that God has these characteristics. They can understand that He is compassionate, protective, gracious, and loving in His discipline.

Some of us had relatively healthy relationships with our parents; others have experienced various forms of neglect, condemnation, and manipulation. Still others have suffered the deeper wounds of sexual abuse, physical abuse, or abandonment. They have not received the parental model of God's character.

The greater the degree of poor modeling in a family, the greater the potential for emotional, spiritual, and relational wounds. If we have been deeply wounded, we may recoil from the truth of God's love instead of being refreshed by it. We may believe that we are unlovable. We may fear reaching out and being hurt again. We may withdraw from the very idea of being loved and accepted.

Think about your understanding of who God is, based on your parents' role modeling. Check the box beside the descriptions that apply.

- ❑ Your father was aloof and distant; therefore, you think of God as someone far away and unreachable.
- ❑ Your mother never was around when you needed her; therefore, it's hard for you to think about God as someone who will be there for you.
- ❑ Your mother never let you forget it when you did something wrong; therefore, it's hard for you to think about God as kind and forgiving.
- ❑ Your father was undependable; therefore, you think of God as someone on whom you can't rely.
- ❑ Your father believed in you and thought you could accomplish anything; therefore, you think of God as someone who has great plans in store for you.
- ❑ Your mother was warm and kind; therefore, it's easy for you to think of God as having compassion.

A Note for Parents

Rejection

1.

2.

3.

4.

5.

Acceptance

1.

2.

3.

4.

5.

In the margin, list one or more techniques that parents use to communicate rejection to children. Then list techniques that communicate acceptance to children.

Parents need to take special note of how they communicate rejection. It may be by verbal attacks on the child's character and abilities, comparisons to other siblings, silence, prolonged absences from home, and physical abuse—actions that carry lifetime scars. That's why many children rebel when they reach adolescence and leave home.

Unconditional acceptance doesn't mean we approve of our children's wrongdoing. Younger children may need confrontation and discipline often. But are we communicating in a godly way, "I love you; I just don't like your misdeed."?

Unconditional acceptance doesn't mean we approve of our children's wrongdoing.

New Models

Persons who have received poor parental modeling need new models—loving Christian friends—to help them experience the love and grace of God. God intends that His body of believers provide us with models of His love, so that our perception of His character slowly can be reshaped into one that is more accurate. This results in a healthier relationship with Him. Then our deep emotional, spiritual, and relational wounds can begin to heal.

If some of you are still looking for a way to more fully experience God's unconditional love, you may need to find a pastor or counselor to help you get started. This person may direct you to one or more believers who can minister to you. A small fellowship group or Bible study is an excellent resource for intimate sharing, comfort, and encouragement. If you have tried to cultivate healthy relationships but haven't found any yet, don't give up! If you ask God for guidance and if you are willing to continue putting forth the effort, He will lead you in His perfect time to persons who can provide a supportive environment for you.

If you need good role models, stop right now and ask for God's guidance. Make a list of persons who might help you. Take this list to your pastor, or a group leader, and ask for his guidance. Your *Search for Significance* group can become a place to find God's love and acceptance. Make your list now and begin to cultivate these relationships.

Recognizing Unhealthy Relationships

We must understand that while God often shows His love and affirmation for us through believers, we all are likely to miss His message and to mistake His messenger(s) as the source of our fulfillment. When this wrong focus is carried to an extreme, we can become emotionally dependent on someone else's presence and/or nurturing for our personal well-being.

Because many of us are so vulnerable when it comes to relationships and the pain that usually accompanies them, we need a basic understanding of healthy and unhealthy relationships. Healthy relationships are turned outward rather than inward. Healthy relationships encourage individuality rather than conformity and independence rather than dependence. Healthy relationships point one's focus toward the Lord and to pleasing Him rather than toward the friendship and pleasing one another.

But how do we know when we've crossed the line from a healthy relationship to one that is emotionally dependent?

As you read the following descriptions, check characteristics that reflect a relationship you currently have.

When either party in a relationship—
- experiences frequent jealousy, possessiveness, and a desire for exclusivism, viewing other persons as a threat to the relationship;
- prefers to spend time alone with this friend and becomes frustrated when this does not happen;
- becomes irrationally angry or depressed when this friend withdraws slightly;
- loses interest in a friendship other than this one;
- has romantic or sexual feelings leading to fantasy about this person;
- becomes preoccupied by the person's appearance, personality, problems, and interests;
- is unwilling to make plans that do not include the other person;
- is unable to see the other's faults realistically;
- becomes defensive about this relationship when someone asks about it;
- displays physical affection beyond what is appropriate for a friendship;
- refers frequently to the other in conversation; feels free to "speak for" the other.

Our relationships with one another are so important to God that He has placed unity among fellow Christians as a priority in our relationship with Him (see Matthew 5:23-24 in the margin). God has reconciled us to Himself as a body in Christ (Ephesians 2:16). Therefore he intends for us to interact as members of one another (Ephesians 4:25).

Pray that God will guide you to relationships that will encourage you to be honest, truthful, and affirming, Ask Him to help you develop an appropriate love for yourself, and focus on Him as the gracious provider of your needs.

Eventually, your gratitude to God will motivate you to practice pleasing Him rather than pleasing other people.

If you are presenting your offering at the altar, and there remember that your brother has something against you, leave your offering there before the altar and go; first to be reconciled to your brother, and then come and present your offering.

Matthew 5:23-24

Day 5

The Free Gift

We can do nothing to contribute to Christ's free gift of salvation; furthermore, if we base our self-worth on others' approval, we actually are saying that their approval is more highly valued than Christ's payment on the cross. We are the sinners, the depraved, the wretched, and the helpless. He is the loving Father, the seeking, searching, patient Savior who has paid for our sins on the cross and has extended to us His grace and sonship.

God seeks us out, convicts us of sin, and reveals Himself to us. God gives us the very faith with which to accept Him. Our faith is simply our response to what He has done for us. Let's look further at what God has done for us.

Read John 5:24 and John 10:27-28. Underline what God has done for you.

Do We Need Other People?

So then, our worth lies in the fact that Christ's blood has paid for our sins; therefore, we are reconciled to God. We are accepted on that basis alone, but does this great truth indicate that we don't need other people in our lives? On the contrary, God very often uses other believers to demonstrate His love and acceptance to us. The strength, comfort, encouragement, and love of Christians toward one another represent a visible expression of God's love.

Sometimes we seem to take it especially hard if fellow Christians do not give us the acceptance and approval we feel we need. Although it's easy to be disappointed when this happens, it truly doesn't matter whether others—Christians or not—accept us. We still are deeply loved, completely forgiven, fully pleasing, totally accepted, and absolutely complete in Christ. He alone is the final authority on our worth and acceptance.

The Biblical Theme of Reconciliation

Continue your study on the theme of reconciliation by reading the Scriptures and by answering these questions.

Acts 10:43: Of what did the prophets bear witness? _____

_____

> Truly, truly, I say to you, he who hears My word, and believes Him who sent Me, has eternal life, and does not come into judgment, but has passed out of death into life,
> John 5:24

> My sheep hear My voice, and I know them, and they follow Me; and I give eternal life to them, and they will never perish; and no one will snatch them out of My hand.
> John 10:27-28

2 Corinthians 5:18-19: _____

_____

You have memorized the first seven lines of "My Identity in Christ." This week add the next three lines. Be prepared to recite this affirmation along with your group.

No Sin Too Filthy!

Is there any sin so filthy that it can prevent a Christian from going to heaven? Absolutely not! A believer is eternally secure; heaven is a certainty for this person. God received us into a loving, intimate, personal relationship the moment we placed our faith in Christ. We are united with God in an eternal and inseparable bond. Reread Romans 8:38-39 in the margin.

Recall the story of Edith on page 71. Although she was a Christian before this event occurred, Edith later stopped attending church because she no longer felt close to God. Although she believed God forgives some sins, she felt that her action was on God's unpardonable list. She spent much of her adult life feeling unworthy of God's love. Only in her senior-adult years did she become convinced of God's unconditional acceptance of her. She later regretted wasting so many critical years of her life that she could have used in God's service.

Do you have any sin in your past or present for which you cannot forgive yourself? Are you not certain God has forgiven you? Do you have a sin that you feel is too filthy to forgive? In the margin write that sin and erase it or totally blot it out. That is what God has done for you.

Can a Christian do anything to become more acceptable to God? If that is the case, what Christ should have said was, "It is almost finished, and if you live a perfect life, you and I together might make you acceptable." No! If such a thing were possible, then the cross would not be enough. If we can do anything to be more acceptable to God, then Christ either lied or was mistaken when He cried out on the cross, "It is finished!" (John 19:30).

Close this week's study with a prayer of thankfulness for Christ's work in making you acceptable to God. Pray that your life will reflect a person freed from the guilt of sin—past and present.

I am convinced that neither death, nor life, nor angels, nor principalities, nor things present, nor things to come, nor powers, 39 nor height, nor depth, nor any other created thing, will be able to separate us from the love of God, which is in Christ Jesus our Lord.

Romans 8:38-39

Week 6
Guilt and Conviction

NO WAY OUT?

Susan was the product of dysfunctional parents. Although she was an attractive child, Susan never seemed quite as confident or as outgoing as her brothers and sisters. Susan's father had sexually abused her by the time she was eight years old. Overcome by the shame this caused her, Susan withdrew from others and looked for an escape.

By age 16 Susan was addicted to drugs and frequently stole merchandise and sold her body for a meager subsistence. Although she was ashamed of her life-style and wanted to change, she saw no way out. The only people who didn't seem to reject her were the ones who used her. Susan felt trapped and alone.

A key verse to memorize this week:

**Fear not, for you will not be put to shame;
And do not feel humiliated, for you will not be disgraced.**
Isaiah 54:4

Words to help you understand this week's lesson:

propitiation (n.)—describes what happened when Christ, through His death, became the means by which God's wrath was satisfied. (*Example:* ***Propitiation*** *demonstrates God's love to people.*)

regeneration (n.)—the renewing work of the Holy Spirit that literally makes each believer experience a new birth the moment he trusts Christ. (*Example:* ***Regeneration*** *took place at our conversion to Christ.*)

Guilt and then conviction are appropriate feelings for a believer who has sinned and wants to restore his or her relationship with

God. Other feelings which masquerade as guilt and conviction pose obstacles and lead to poor self-esteem. This week we will look at the difference.

Day 1
Guilt and Condemnation

No feeling produces pain, fear, and alienation quite like guilt. Many of us know it as a constant burden. Some of us respond to it like a whipped puppy, beaten down and ashamed. Some of us avoid it through the numbing effects of denial.

Guilt causes a loss of self-respect. It withers the human spirit and eats away at our personal significance. Guilt is a strong motivation,playing on our fears of failure and rejection; therefore, it can never ultimately build, encourage, or inspire us in our desire to live for Christ.

Our guilt may be prompted by many factors: poor parental modeling of Christ's love and forgiveness, divorce, neglect, a particular past sin, or the emphasis some believers place on the oughts and shoulds of Christianity. Regardless of these influences, guilt need not be a way of life for us.

> There is now no condemnation for those who are in Christ Jesus.
> Romans 8:1

Read Romans 8:1. When I shared this important truth with a troubled Christian brother, his jaw dropped and his eyes filled with tears. He looked at me and exclaimed, "You mean, all this guilt I have been carrying for so long is unnecessary? I can be free from these tormenting feelings of condemnation? Why hasn't somebody told me this before?"

The apostle Paul has been trying to tell us just that for centuries, but few of us have listened. We feel we deserve condemnation, and we fail to realize that Christ has freed us from the guilt and condemnation our sins deserve.

Guilt has a restricted meaning in the New Testament. It refers to humankind's condition prior to salvation. Only the non-Christian is actually guilty before God. He has transgressed the law of God and must face the consequences. Guilt shakes its fist and says, "You have fallen short and must pay the price. You are personally accountable."

The impact of Romans 8:1 is that the believer is released from the law and its condemnation. This does not mean we are without standards of conduct. Sin is naturally destructive. It does mean that our failing to meet these standards does not bring eternal separation from God.

Whether consciously or unconsciously, we all tend to cover our failure by pointing an accusing finger. More often than not, we can find no one but ourselves to blame, so the accusing finger points right back at us. Self-condemnation is a severe form of punishment.

As you read the next paragraph, underline the ways you talk to yourself when you are punishing yourself for a misdeed. Circle the ways you talk to others when you feel they are to blame.

Self-condemnation may include name-calling *(I'm so stupid! I can't do anything right!)*, making jokes or statements at our own expense, or simply never allowing any room for error in our performance. With others we may be harsh (physically or verbally abusive) or relatively subtle (sarcastic or silent). But any form of condemnation is a powerfully destructive force that communicates, *I'll make you sorry for what you did.*

Our condemnation—whether from ourselves or others— is removed only through Christ. He took all our guilt on Himself when He accepted the penalty for our sins and suffered the full punishment for all sin. Because of His substitution, we need never face guilt's ultimate consequences. We are acquitted and absolved from guilt, free from our sentence of spiritual death.

> **Christ accepted the penalty for our sins and suffered the full punishment for all sin.**

Perhaps some people think that if they don't use guilt for motivation, we won't do anything. Guilt may motivate us for a short while. The long-term results of grace best motivate us because they come from the inside out.

Loving friends who listen to us and encourage us can be an example of God's forgiveness to us. As we become more honest about our feelings through these affirming relationships, we will be able to experience increasingly the freedom, forgiveness, and freshness of God's grace.

Memorize the last five lines from "My Identity in Christ." Practice saying them out loud. You will say them with your group when you meet again.

The Greatest Act of Love

Because God is the Almighty, the rightful judge of the universe, absolutely holy and perfect, He cannot overlook sin, nor can He compromise by accepting sinful behavior. For God to condone even one sin would mar His holiness. It would be like smearing a white wedding gown with black tar.

Propitiation refers to Christ's death on the cross, which satisfied, or took care of, the penalty for our sins. Christ's death propitiates, or does away with, God's anger. God's righteous anger is directed against all sin and, therefore, against all sinful people. Christ's death removed God's anger from those who are sorry and turn away from their sins.

Check each of the statements below that helps explain the meaning of *propitiation*.
   ❏ 1. Christ's death was a substitution for my sins.
   ❏ 2. My sin deserves God's anger.
   ❏ 3. I must pay for my own sins.
   ❏ 4. Christ paid for my sin penalty.
   ❏ 5. Christ's death does away with God's anger.

Sending His Son to die on the cross was the most loving act in all of history.

Most of us have experienced acts of kindness done for us. What God did for us, however, in sending His Son to die on the cross was the most loving act in all of history.

Pray, thanking God for His great love and for Christ's payment on the cross for our sins. Then pray the words of "My Identity in Christ" as a statement of your value to God and others.

Day 2

Blame and Propitiation

Success or failure is often the main way we evaluate ourselves and others. If we believe that failure makes us unacceptable and unworthy of love, then we usually feel completely justified in condemning those who fail, including ourselves.

No Right to Feel Good

Matt made a serious mistake early in his life and never was able to overcome it. At age 14 he and several friends from school stepped inside a downtown department store and tried to slip out with some cassette tapes without paying for them. They made it to the glass doors past the cashier's stand before a security guard caught them and escorted all of them to the manager's office.

Matt never heard the end of the incident. Every time he made a mistake at home, his father reminded him of what he had done. "You're a colossal failure!" his father screamed. "You've got no values whatsoever! You're a liar and a thief, and you'll never amount to anything!"

Matt never was able to forget his humiliation. At age 20 he sat in my office and very seriously told me that on some days he discovered that he actually was happy until he realized that he was feeling good. Believing he had no right to feel good about himself, he then began to feel depressed. "After all," he reflected, "no one as worthless as I am has a right to feel happy."

In the margin describe a time you experienced some type of humiliation that made you feel unworthy of love.

The Search for a Culprit

For most of our lives, we have been conditioned to make someone pay for failures or shortcomings. When someone misses a deadline at work, we let everyone know it's not our fault. If someone leaves a household chore undone, we quickly look to our other family members to determine who is responsible. We hope to clear ourselves from blame by making sure that others properly identify and punish the one who failed. Blaming others also helps put a safe distance between their failure and our fragile self-worth.

Check the reasons you may have used to assign blame for past failures.

- ❏ I punish myself for past failures so I won't do it again.
- ❏ I blame others for past failures to relieve my conscience.
- ❏ I defend myself by blaming failure on others.
- ❏ Blaming others makes me feel better about myself.

Rather than looking for a biblical solution to our problems, we blame others to make ourselves feel better. By blaming someone else who failed, we feel superior. In fact, the higher the position of the one who failed (CEO, government figure, boss, and so on), the farther they fall and often, the better we feel. This desire to be "one up" on someone is at the root of gossip.

Stop and pray, asking God to help you have an open mind about blame. Ask Him to help you understand why you often are determined to blame yourself or others.

Many of us take great steps to cover for others, even if that means accepting blame for them when they're clearly at fault. This is one reason why denial is so strong in abusive families.

Think of a close friend or family member with whom you had a conflict. Check your most usual response when you want to punish that person because of the conflict.

- ❏ Withdraw love, affection, and encouragement
- ❏ Make sarcastic remarks
- ❏ Speak to him or her abruptly
- ❏ Abuse him or her verbally or physically
- ❏ Give the person the silent treatment for several days
- ❏ Get even through a harmful deed to the person

People react in these ways because they believe that failure must be punished instead of forgiven. You even may have appointed yourself to carry out the sentence of punishment.

Believing You Must Pay

After reading about blame, some people immediately recognize that they automatically respond this way. Others are blind to it. You may think this false belief does not affect you at all, but it probably does.

You may think this false belief does not affect you at all, but it probably does.

Check the statement you find to be true in your own life.
- ❏ When something fails, I generally have an urge to blame someone else.
- ❏ When something fails, I generally take the blame.
- ❏ When I fail, I look for excuses.

If one or both of these is true about you, then you need to recognize that this false belief—someone is to blame and must be punished— has a controlling effect on your life.

Tom was becoming an emotional zombie under his wife's constant condemnation, but instead of fighting back, he kept thinking, *Yes, Suzanne's right. I am an incompetent fool.* He attacked himself over and over so that he became like the worn-out punching bag of a heavyweight fighter. Rather than working out their problems and objectively evaluating their actions, Suzanne blamed Tom, and Tom blamed himself.

We think that if we feel badly enough for long enough (the severity and length depending, of course, on how large the sin is), the sin will be forgiven and we can go on with life. No one likes to be punished, so if you believe that God's attitude toward you is anger and condemnation, you will try to avoid Him. But God has demonstrated His love for us on the cross when Christ paid our sins in full. Therefore, God doesn't punish us for our sins. Christ bore that punishment on the cross.

And to think, God did it for people who have hurt Him mightily since the beginning of creation! God has seen His children rebel against the God of love and peace. If we don't act with a desire to glorify Him, even "good" deeds are like filthy garments to God.

In His holiness God condemns sin, but in the most awesome example of love the world ever has seen, He decided that His Son would die to pay for our sins. God sacrificed the sinless, perfect Savior to turn away—to propitiate—His great wrath.

Write the third of Satan's lies and God's truth that defeats it (see p. 128).

Those who fail _____

_____

_____

Because of propitiation _____

_____

Day 3
Shame and Regeneration

Some of us base our self-worth on past failures; others are dissatisfied with personal appearance; bad habits defeats many. As a result, we often develop a fourth false belief: *I am what I am. I cannot change. I am hopeless.* This lie binds people to pessimism—or the belief that things can't get better.

"I just can't help myself," some people say. "That's the way I've always been, and that's the way I'll always be. You can't teach an old dog new tricks." We assume that others should have low expectations of us, too. "You know I can't do any better than that. What do you expect?"

In the margin list things about your appearance or past performance that you have tried to change in order to feel better about yourself.

Stuck like Glue to the Past
When Leslie approached Janet about serving a term as the president of the Ladies' Auxiliary, Janet's outward poise and confidence vanished. "Are you serious?" she stuttered. "You know I've never been a leader and have never even gotten along well with people. No, no, I'd simply embarrass you. No, I can't do it, don't you see?"

Janet 's opinion of herself was based on her past failures. Those failures kept her from enjoying new experiences. If you are evaluating yourself by your past performance or appearance, you are viewing yourself incorrectly. Recognize that God has made you into a new creature through Christ's death on the cross. God says you are deeply loved, fully pleasing, completely forgiven, and totally accepted by Him and absolutely complete in Christ.

shame (n.)—a painful emotion caused by awareness of guilt, short-comings, or improper behavior, a condition of humiliating disgrace

Shame (read its definition in the margin) can have a tremendous impact on us if we believe that we never can be different from what we have been. Left in this hopeless state, we likely will feel trapped in helplessness about ourselves and our future.

Because what we do is based on our self-concept, our every action reinforces a positive or negative view of ourselves. Shame often occurs when we consider a failure in our performance or a flaw in our appearance so important that it creates a permanently negative opinion about our self-worth.

All of us have become like one who is unclean, and all our righteous deeds are like a filthy garment; and all of us wither like a leaf, and our iniquities, like the wind, take us away.
Isaiah 64:6

Write the fourth false belief.

I am what _____

Too often, our self-image rests solely on how we look at our past behavior. We end up measuring ourselves only through a memory. Day after day, year after year we tend to build our personalities on yesterday's personal disappointments.

A young man named Jeff once questioned me when I told him that he needed to separate his past from the present. I told him that no law required him to remain the same individual he always had been. I told Jeff that he could rise above his past and build a new life for himself. "But how?" Jeff asked. "I'm more of a realist than that. I know myself. I know what I've done and who I am. I've tried to change, but it hasn't worked. I've given up now."

How would you have answered Jeff if you were his counselor? Write your answer in the margin.

I explained to Jeff that he needed a new perspective, not just new efforts, based on the unconditional love and acceptance of God. Both Jeff's past failures and God's unconditional love were realities. The question, however, was this: Which one would Jeff value more? If he continued to value his failures, he would continue to be caught up in self-pity.

Instead, Jeff needed to be honest. He needed someone with whom he could talk openly so that he could express his feelings without fearing rejection. And he needed someone to encourage him to study and to apply the truths of God's Word.

If he continues at this process, his sense of self-worth will begin to change. Jeff eventually will experience changes in every area: his goals, his relationships, and his outlook. Nothing forces us to remain in the mold of the past. By the grace and power of God, we can change! We can persevere and overcome!

Releasing the Old Trapeze Bar
Paul Tournier once compared life to the experience of a man hanging from a trapeze. The trapeze bar was the man's security, his lifestyle. Then God swung another trapeze into the man's view, and the man faced a confusing dilemma. Should he give up his past? Should he reach for the new bar? Tournier explained that the moment of truth came when the man realized that to grab the new bar, he must release the old one.

In our past relationships we may have experienced failure in a meaningful aspect of our character or actions. If we do not begin the process of letting go, however, we will be unable to experience the joy and the challenge of the present. We also will be unable to be realistic about the possibility of failure again.

Perhaps we find a strange kind of comfort in our personal failings. Perhaps we find security in accepting ourselves as much less than we can become. That reduces the risk of failure considerably. Certainly, if we expect little from ourselves, we seldom will be disappointed!

Which of these events or situations have been the most significant to the development of your self-worth?
- ❏ What parents have said or done to me
- ❏ What friends have said or done to me
- ❏ What I say about myself
- ❏ What a teacher or supervisor has said or done to me
- ❏ Others: _____

God's Answer: Regeneration

If you are evaluating yourself by your past performance or appearance, you are viewing yourself incorrectly. Recognize that God has made you a new creature through Christ's death on the cross. God says you are deeply loved, fully pleasing, completely forgiven, totally accepted by Him, and absolutely complete in Christ.

regeneration (n.)—the renewing work of the Holy Spirit that literally makes each believer experience a new birth the moment he trusts Christ. (Example: Regeneration took place at our conversion to Christ.)

God's answer to shame is ***regeneration***, not a self-improvement program nor a clean-up campaign for our sinful natures. Regeneration is nothing less than the giving of new life. As Paul stated in Ephesians 2:5, "Even when we were dead in our transgressions, [God] made us alive together with Christ." In his letter to the young pastor Titus, Paul also wrote about this incredible transformation process:

In that wondrous, miraculous moment when we trust Christ, we experience a renewal of the human spirit. This transformation takes place so that the Spirit lives in us. Read Romans 8:10.

Christ is in you, though the body is dead because of sin, yet the spirit is alive because of righteousness.
Romans 8:10

Describe how you feel when you realize that Christ's Spirit lives in you.

_____

_____

Complete in Christ

In the church at Colossae, false teachers taught that completeness comes through a combination of philosophy, good works, other religions, and Christ. Paul's clear message was that we are made complete through Christ alone.

Nothing can add to the death of Christ to pay for our sins, and nothing can add to the resurrection of Christ to give us new life. We are complete because Christ has forgiven us and given us life—the capacity for growth and change.

Write below the fourth false belief and God's truth.

I am what _____

_____

Because of regeneration _____

_____

In Him [Christ] all fullness of Deity dwells in bodily form, and in Him you have been made complete, and He is the head over all rule and authority.

Colossians 2:9-10

Day 4
Guilt vs. Conviction

Recall from day 1 that many Christians equate any guilt with condemnation. Condemnation and conviction are not the same. In fact, they are actually worlds apart. Condemnation refers to what our sin deserves. Conviction is the privilege of believers, given by the Holy Spirit, to repent of their sins and pray for forgiveness. Guilt brings depression and despair, but conviction enables us to realize the beauty of God's forgiveness and to experience His love and power.

Learn to identify false guilt (something we have put on ourselves) from true guilt, manifested by conviction from the Holy Spirit. Christians are freed from guilt, but we are still subject to conviction. The Bible frequently speaks of the Holy Spirit's work to convict believers of sin. He directs and encourages our spiritual progress by revealing our sins in contrast to the holiness and purity of Christ.

Although the Holy Spirit convicts both believers and unbelievers of sin (John 16:8), His conviction of believers deals with our behavior, not our status before God. Conviction is the Holy Spirit's way of showing the error of our performance in light of God's standard and truth. His motivation is love, correction, and protection.

Perhaps these statements will better illustrate the contrasting purposes and results of guilt and conviction:

• **Basic focus:** Guilt focuses on the state of being condemned: "I am unworthy." Conviction focuses on behavior: "This act is unworthy of Christ and is destructive."

- **Primary concern:** Guilt deals with the sinner's loss of self-esteem and a wounded self-pride: "What will others think of me?" Conviction deals with the loss of our moment-by-moment communication with God: "This act is destructive to me and interferes with my walk with God."
- **Primary fear:** Guilt produces a fear of punishment: "Now I'm going to get it!" Conviction produces a fear of the destructiveness of the act itself: "This behavior is destructive to me and others, and it robs me of what God intends for me."
- **Agent:** The agent of guilt is Satan: "The god of this world has blinded the minds of the unbelieving so that they might not see the light of the gospel of the glory of Christ" (2 Corinthians 4:4). The agent of conviction is the Holy Spirit: "If by the Spirit you are putting to death the deeds of the body, you will live" (Romans 8:13).
- **Behavioral results:** Guilt leads to depression and more sin: "I am just a low-down, dirty, rotten sinner;" or to rebellion: "I don't care. I'm going to do whatever I want to do." Conviction leads to repentance, the turning from sin to Christ: "Lord, I agree with You that my sin is wrong and destructive. Show me your way."
- **Interpersonal result:** The interpersonal result of guilt is alienation, a feeling of shame that drives one away from the person who has been wronged: "I can't ever face him or her again." The interpersonal result of conviction is restoration, a desire to remedy the harm done to others: "Father, what would You have me do to right this wrong and restore the relationship with the one I have offended?"
- **Personal results:** Guilt ends in depression, bitterness, and self-pity: "I'm just no good." Conviction ends in the realization of forgiveness: "You have made me complete and have given me the righteousness of Christ, even though my performance often falls short.

As we yield to the gentle prodding of God-given conviction, confess our sins, and affirm our true relationship with Him, we will be gradually shaped and molded in such a way that we will increasingly honor the one who died and rose again on our behalf.

Refuse then to believe Satan's lies any longer, and focus instead on the unconditional love and forgiveness of Christ. His love is powerful, and He is worthy of our intense zeal to obey and honor Him. The result of proper motivation is an enduring, deepening commitment to Christ and His cause.

We also once were foolish ourselves, disobedient, deceived, enslaved to various lusts and pleasures, spending our life in malice and envy, hateful, hating one another. But when the kindness of God our Savior and His love for mankind appeared, He saved us, not on the basis of deeds which we have done in righteousness, but according to His mercy, by the washing of regeneration and renewing by the Holy Spirit, whom He poured out upon us richly through Jesus Christ our Savior, so that being justified by His grace we might be made heirs according to the hope of eternal life.

Titus 3:3-7

Confess and Get on with Life

When we sin, we can follow King David's example. When Nathan confronted David about his sin of adultery with Bathsheba, David confessed his sin to the Lord (2 Samuel 12:1-13). David did not run from his sin or its consequences. He did not deny it, nor did he hide from it. He married Bathsheba, who gave birth to Solomon, who became the wise king of Israel.

Certainly, God could have brought Solomon into the world another way; but perhaps as a message to us, He chose Bathsheba as the mother. What a message! Confess your sins, worship God, and get on with your life. You can experience the mercy of God no matter what you've done or been through.

Pray this prayer or one of your own to God right now.

Lord, I confess my sins to You. (List them. Be specific.) I agree with You that these things are wrong. I also agree that they have been destructive to my life. Thank You for Your grace and forgiveness. Is there anything I need to return, anyone I need to repay, or anyone I need to apologize to? Thank You. Amen.

Day 5
Forgiving at a Deeper Level

Now that we have seen the effects of blame and shame, we must take seriously God's offer of propitiation and regeneration. Regeneration gives us a new beginning. We no longer have to think, feel, and act in the way false beliefs dictate. We are free to present ourselves to God as an instrument of righteousness. This process is a life-time commitment which involves three steps:

- **Lay aside the old self**—rejecting the old self's hold on how you think, feel, and act; choosing to stop living in worldliness.
- **Renew your mind with God's truth**—understanding what Christ has accomplished for you and how that gives you a new capacity to live for Him.
- **Put on the new self**—let the Holy Spirit guide in your thoughts, words, actions, values, and relationships.

Ephesians 4:24 says that our new self has been created in righteousness and holiness, but we must yet put on this new self in order to produce godly thoughts and actions over time—as the verses in the margin indicate.

Read the verses in the margin. Cross through any of these words that do not represent the new self.

Holy	Angry	Peaceful	Deceptive	Impatient
Kind	Forgiving	Humble	Prideful	Loving

It is written, "You shall be holy, for I am holy."

1 Peter 1:16

As those who have been chosen of God, holy and beloved, put on a heart of compassion, kindness, humility, gentleness and patience; bearing with one another, and forgiving each other, whoever has a complaint against anyone; just as the Lord forgave you, so also should you. Beyond all these things put on love, which is the perfect bond of unity. Let the peace of Christ rule in your hearts, to which indeed you were called in one body; and be thankful.

Colossians 3:12-15

Old habits—though hard to shake—can be overcome. As hurts from our past continue to surface, we often need to begin learning how to forgive at a deeper level.

forgiveness (n.)—the act of ceasing to feel resentment against (an offender) … the granting of relief from payment of a debt (Webster's)

Read the definition of *forgiveness* in the margin. Below it write what forgiveness means to you.

Forgiveness is always a decision—usually a difficult one. Forgiveness is counting the cost and releasing others from the debt they owe. If I really release you from this debt, I'll resist the urge to remind you about it. If I am to forgive you, I must release you from even the guilt of the penalty you would have owed me. Then I must release you from the penalty itself. At this point I may be tempted to indulge in self-pity, hatred, bitterness, and depression. I may also want to seek revenge.

In your Bible read the following Scriptures: Matthew 6:15; Mark 11:25; Ephesians 4:32. Check three reasons the Bible gives to show why we should forgive.

❏ 1. An unforgiving spirit hurts us.
❏ 2. We will profit financially if we forgive.
❏ 3. God commands us to forgive others.
❏ 4. God has forgiven us through Jesus Christ.
❏ 5. People will accept us if we forgive them.
❏ 6. Forgiving will cause us to perform better.

Until we can truly understand how great our own sin is and how much grief it brings to God and others, we neither can fully appreciate nor fully experience how much it cost Christ to forgive us. Understanding how deep His forgiveness is toward us provides us with the compassion, mercy, and motivation to forgive others.

Check the statements below that show what effect our reconciliation to God has in our lives.

❏ Christ has avenged the righteous wrath of God for our sins.
❏ We are not justified in God's sight.
❏ We are justified in God's sight and are fully pleasing to Him despite our sin.
❏ We are reconciled to our Creator through the sacrifice of His blood.
❏ We can enjoy intimate fellowship with Him.

If we are willing to forgive others, that willingness assures us that God is working in our lives through His Holy Spirit and that we are, indeed, recipients of His generous mercy and forgiveness. As we become reconciled to a previous offender, we will grasp how important it is that we are reconciled to God through Christ. If offenders are not believers, God may use our forgiveness as a way to bring them to a trusting relationship with Him.

Reread Matthew 6:15 (p. 96). Unwillingness to forgive has consequences. If the person who has injured you is unaware of the harm he or she has caused you, he or she may be confused by your behavior. Besides feeling alienated from you, this person may experience deep anxiety about you and your relationship.

Read Romans 12:14. Underline what it teaches about how you should treat someone who has harmed you.

> Bless those who persecute you; bless and do not curse.
>
> Romans 12:14

Harvey's boss, Derrick, fired him two days after assuring Harvey that he had a bright future with the company. Harvey had left a secure job he had held for 10 years to take the position with Derrick's company. He had uprooted his family and left behind many friends. Now he was unemployed. The next several years were nightmares for Harvey as he struggled to find new employment and to support his family. Harvey wondered if he ever could forgive Derrick.

Gradually, after much prayer and allowing God to speak to him through His Word, Harvey found that he was able to forgive his former boss. He never forgot the incident, but Harvey was able to distinguish between Derrick and his harmful behavior.

Eventually, when we forgive, our thoughts about the person who harmed us increasingly can be characterized by love and compassion; and we can extend a blessing rather than an insult to him or her.

It's time for a quick refresher course on your memory work on the affirmation "My Identity in Christ." Review the entire affirmation and repeat it again from memory.

Week 7

The Trip In

A CAREER DOWN THE TUBE?

John, a chronic alcoholic, completed a substance-abuse treatment program and wisely made sobriety his absolute priority. However, business pressures distracted him to the point he thought he must resign his executive job to stay sober. A promising career was about to go right down the tube.

Rather than give in to his painful emotions and resign from his job, the Holy Spirit helped John act consistently with a belief in his self-worth based on Jesus. When John separated his personal worth from his job performance, he began to enjoy his job once again. Quiet confidence came as John began to act and live out what he believed about himself.

A key verse to memorize this week:

If anyone is a hearer of the word and not a doer, he is like a man who looks at his natural face in a mirror; for once he has looked at himself and gone away, he has immediately forgotten what kind of person he was.

James 1:23-24

Words to help you understand this week's lessons:

repress (v.)—to prevent the natural or normal expression, activity, or develop ment of. *(Example: We may have learned to **repress** painful emotions.)*

The Trip In (n.)—a look inside yourself in a special, deliberate way to enable you to correct the false beliefs causing your painful emotions and then replace them with God's truth. (Example: Persons can use The Trip In to reject false beliefs that cause painful feelings and to embrace God's truth.) **See diagram on page 112.**

How do we combine what we have learned about Satan's lies and God's truth with thoughts and actions that will make a difference in our lives? This final week you'll learn to take The Trip In by looking inside yourself, rejecting a false belief, and acting on the basis of God's truth. If you believe you are a loved and forgiven child of God, you will have found the key to personal significance. Now it is up to you to use that key.

Day 1
Getting Ready for the Journey

Believe it or not, desire it or not, understand it or not, we are at war. The Scriptures in the margin tell about this warfare. Most of us don't like to think about Satan having a role in our lives. We hope the war will pass us by, but we can't avoid these battles. Our minds are the battlefield for this warfare (see Romans 12:2).

Satan seeks to keep our minds as they are so we won't be transformed. He establishes fortresses of deception. A fortress is a high, strong barrier such as a wall around a city. This wall protects thoughts that go against the knowledge or understanding of God. We are deceived by our belief systems that we reinforce over the years by the thoughts, emotions, and actions that produce lack of self worth. These are self-feeding systems; in other words, we do this to ourselves!

Let's look at what happens when a person who normally believes she is a failure succeeds at something. When she succeeds, her belief system (her fortress) produces thoughts like the following. As you read, circle statements you have thought about yourself in similar situations.

If she succeeds, her belief system produces thoughts:
- What luck!
- It's about time. Look at all the failure I've had to go through just to get one success.
- How unusual for a loser like me to do something right!

If the person fails, her belief system produces thoughts:
- I told you I would fail.
- What a loser I am!
- I can't help it; I just can't do any better.

Underline thoughts similar to your own.

Though we walk in the flesh, we do not war according to the flesh, for the weapons of our warfare are not of the flesh, but divinely powerful for the destruction of fortresses. We are destroying speculations and every lofty thing raised up against the knowledge of God, and we are taking every thought captive to the obedience of Christ.

2 Corinthians 10:3-5

Be transformed by the renewing of your mind, so that you may prove what the will of God is, that which is good and acceptable and perfect.

Romans 12:2

Whether she succeeds or fails, the result is the same. It merely reinforces her belief that she is mostly a failure.

Establishing a Stronghold of Truth

You can learn to use the following practices to begin to establish a stronghold of truth in your mind. We must renew our minds to reject Satan's lies and replace them with God's truths.

The Truth Card

The "My Identity in Christ" statement can be a key factor in helping you base your self-worth on the freeing truths of the Scriptures.

1. To make a Truth Card, use a three-by-five-inch card. On the front write the following truths and their corresponding verses from Scripture.
   - I am deeply loved by God (1 John 4:9-10).
   - I am completely forgiven and fully pleasing to God (Romans 5:1).
   - I am totally accepted by God (Colossians 1:21-22).
   - I am a new creation, absolutely complete in Christ (2 Corinthians 5:17).

   On the back of the card, write the false beliefs appearing on page 128.

2. Carry this card with you continuously. For one month, each time you do a routine activity, like drinking your morning cup of coffee, look at the front side and slowly meditate on each phrase. Thank the Lord for making you into a person with these qualities. By doing this exercise for the next month, you can develop a habit of remembering you are deeply loved, completely forgiven, fully pleasing, totally accepted, and absolutely complete in Christ.

Let the word of Christ richly dwell within you, with all wisdom teaching and admonishing one another with psalms and hymns and spiritual songs, singing with thankfulness in your hearts to God.

Colossians 3:16

If you have not already done so, during the next four days memorize the verses listed on the card. Look in your Bible for other verses that support these truths. Memorizing these verses will establish God's Word as the basis for your beliefs. Let God speak to you through them, as the verse in the margin instructs you to do. Also memorize the false beliefs. The more familiar you are with these lies, the more likely you are to recognize them in your thoughts. As you recognize them, you can replace them with the truths of God's Word.

The Trip In

Your ability to correct the false beliefs that cause your harmful emotions and destructive behavior will depend on the way you learn to look within yourself. You can learn to do this in a special, deliberate way. Read **The Trip In** on page 112. Then return to this page in day 1.

Your beliefs usually influence your thoughts, emotions, and actions. False beliefs are Satan's lies, and they generate ungodly thoughts, painful emotions, and sinful actions. You no longer have to think, feel, and act in the way false beliefs dictate.

In your own words, explain The Trip In as though you were telling it to someone new in your group.

_____

_____

_____

_____

Read the summary in the margin. Identify the step you feel will be the most difficult for you to accomplish. Underline it. Then stop and pray, asking God to help you accomplish it.

During the next four days we will discuss each step in detail.

Do these things in a Trip In:
- Identify destructive behavior.
- Discover the trigger emotion.
- Detect the false beliefs.
- Reject the false beliefs.
- Affirm the truth about your worth. Act accordingly!

Day 2
Step 1: What Do I Feel?

When a situation bothers you, The Trip In provides a process to get in touch with what you really feel. Your first step is to identify the painful emotions causing your destructive thoughts or behavior. In any given situation you could experience several painful emotions. You need to identify all of them you're feeling and filter through them until you detect the one that underlies all the others. Otherwise, you would have only a surface analysis.

Some emotions, such as anger and hatred, are sharp, clearly felt, and easily labeled. But underlying emotions such as fear and shame often are unclear until you focus on them deliberately.

A college student once focused on his feelings about his father. As he took the Trip In, he at first decided he felt *angry* about his father. Then, as he thought some more, he decided that instead of anger, the correct description of how he felt actually might be *resentment*. Although he knew he was getting close, the student tried to probe even more deeply to identify his emotion correctly. He next considered the feeling of being *neglected* as he tried to zero in on the precise emotion. Finally he realized that what he really felt was *abandonment and the fear of being abandoned again*. His father left him feeling totally abandoned; that was the emotion underlying all the others.

Now You Try It

When you look inside yourself to examine the painful emotions you feel about a particular situation, do these things:

1. Find a place where you will not be interrupted.

2. Shut everything else out. Concentrate on how you feel about the situation.

3. Think of the single feeling at the root of your emotional response to the situation. Don't try to analyze the problem. You are trying to get to the underlying emotion prompting your response to the situation.

Filter through all the painful emotions you're feeling until you detect the one that underlies the others.

As you begin to focus, you might sense a number of emotions. Make note of all you feel. One of the most important techniques for focusing is to ask yourself questions such as the ones below.

What is the worst thing about this situation? _____

_____

How does it affect me personally? _____

_____

What is the main problem in it that makes me feel bad?
_____

Describe the worst part of this feeling. _____

_____

Take your time and concentrate. Let the awareness of your feeling come to you naturally; don't force it. Be honest about your emotions. You may think you have arrived at the underlying emotion before you actually do. The search can be like hide-and-seek when someone says *Cold, colder, ice cold* if you are moving in the wrong direction or *Warm, warmer, red hot* as you move in the right direction. Take your time. Move through your feelings until you gain an insight of the underlying emotion that you feel.

Sometimes we have a difficult time identifying our emotions because we have learned to **repress** painful emotions. We repress emotions because we fear confronting them. Some of us have become numb, unable to feel either anger or joy, hurt or love. As a defense mechanism we forget, minimize, or deny painful emotions—claiming they really didn't hurt. Learning to identify our feelings allows us to use them to determine if our response to a situation is based on the truth or a lie.

repress (v.)—to prevent the natural or normal expression, activity, or development of; to exclude from consciousness (Webster's)

How can you know when you discover the emotion at the root of a situation? The more you take The Trip In, the more easily you can tell when you arrive at the underlying emotion because you often experience a feeling of release.

How can you know?

Think about a time when you sensed that you'd forgotten something. *What did I forget?* you ask yourself as you probe for the answer. No matter how much you tell yourself not to worry, the feeling keeps nagging at you. Then, suddenly, what you forgot bursts to the surface of your mind. You remember, *I forgot to bring the contracts*. The realization gives you a sudden sense of relief. This is the key characteristic when you identify the underlying emotion you feel. It's like exhaling after holding your breath— "That's it! I found it!" You then can begin to resolve the hurts that cause the emotion.

A "That's it! I found it!" feeling

Three main benefits exist from zeroing in on the underlying emotion you feel in a bothersome situation.
1. You can be honest about the realities of a situation and your response to it.
2. You can grieve the sense of loss you feel.
3. You can take responsibility for your choices and behaviors.

Think of a recent painful situation. Try to focus on the underlying emotion you felt. As you focus, study the words listed at the top of page 104. Then see if you can isolate one feeling that seems to represent the underlying emotion you felt. Put a check beside that emotion.

❏ Abandoned   ❏ Forgotten   ❏ Neglected
❏ Angry   ❏ Humiliated   ❏ Ostracized
❏ Betrayed   ❏ Ignored   ❏ Perplexed
❏ Confused   ❏ Lonely   ❏ Ridiculed
❏ Excluded   ❏ Misunderstood   ❏ Unappreciated
❏ Afraid   ❏ Disgusted   ❏ Resentful
❏ _____

Day 3

Step 2: Why Do I Feel It?

Once you have discovered the emotions that you feel in a distressing situation, you can venture still deeper within to ask yourself, *Why do I feel this way? What are the false beliefs causing my painful feelings?* The diagram on page 128 can help you identify some common false beliefs.

By asking, *Why do I feel it?* you can go behind your painful emotions to identify the specific false beliefs causing them. To help you detect your false beliefs, think through the following questions about what you are feeling. We refer to this set of questions as The Why Formula.

THE WHY FORMULA

- Why am I feeling this way? I must be taking this situation personally for it to make me feel this badly.

- What are the specific false beliefs about myself that are causing my painful feelings?

In earlier chapters you studied the four false beliefs. Almost every destructive behavior has one of these four false beliefs as the root cause.

Letting the Formula Work for You

Bill overslept and was late for an important meeting. Bill prided himself on being prompt, so this incident greatly embarrassed him. When Bill walked into the meeting his boss chided him, and he became flustered as his coworkers glared at him. One of Bill's coworkers made a sarcastic remark. Bill felt as if a harsh spotlight focused directly on him. He felt exposed and humiliated as a result. Bill quickly took a seat at the table.

Bill was tempted to react like they did. After all, he was rarely late. But, he was late, and he had to take the responsibility for failing to get out of bed. After an appropriate apology, Bill expected to feel better, but he didn't. Fortunately Bill had learned about taking The Trip In to see why this situation bothered him so much.

First, Bill focused on his emotions. He asked himself, *What do I really feel? What emotions are causing my destructive behavior?* As he began to sift through his emotions, he discovered he felt anxiety about his boss' chiding and his coworkers' glares. Then he realized that he felt humiliated. Finally, he discovered that the most intense emotion he felt was personal failure. After he discovered this emotion, he completed The Trip In by focusing on the false beliefs causing his painful emotion. He applied The Why Formula by asking himself, *Why am I feeling this way? I must be taking this situation personally for it to make me feel this badly. What are the false beliefs which cause me to feel this way?*

As he progressed from the questions in The Why Formula to the four false beliefs, Bill detected the false belief causing his reaction to being late. Bill recognized how the belief influenced him and said to himself, *I have the false belief that I must be adequate and achieve in my performance to have self-worth. That is precisely why it depresses me when my boss and others snipe and glare at me when I'm late. Since I believe I have self-worth when I feel I'm prompt and prepared, I set myself up to feel like a failure when someone criticizes my performance.*

In the margin apply The Why Formula, as Bill did, to the situation you identified for yourself on page 103.

Note that Bill's proper response was not, *I'm not anxious. I don't feel like a failure* when, in fact, he did feel that way. Denial only compounds our problems; it's not a solution. We can be honest about our feelings.

Instead of blaming his boss and his coworkers, Bill began taking responsibility for his reaction. The real cause of his anxiety was his own false belief. Once Bill began rejecting his false belief and affirming his worth as a person, he conquered his hypersensitivity at his job. Bill simply refused to take their scolding, stares, and snipes as a reflection on his character.

The Why Formula

Write your answers below.

1. _____

_____

2. _____

_____

Look back through the story of Bill and the embarrassing meeting. Underline statements about Bill's feelings that remind you of similar pain you felt in uncomfortable situations. Ask yourself, *To what false beliefs can I trace my painful emotions?* Then stop and pray that God will help you learn to make The Why Formula second nature in your life to help you overcome painful feelings.

Day 4

Step 3: What Do I Believe?

Once you really get in touch with what you feel about a situation and trace your emotions back to the false beliefs causing them, you can begin consciously and boldly to reject your false beliefs. Recognizing your false beliefs does not necessarily change you unless you declare war on them. Refuse to live by those false beliefs! Seek to remove them from your mind!

Bill saw that he held to the false belief that he must achieve to feel good about himself as a person. Bill declared war on his false belief. Bill was determined to stop his pattern of believing lies about himself and his situation. Bill rejected his false belief as he declared to himself, *I admit the fact that I am taking this personally because I wrongly hold to the false belief that I must achieve in my performance to feel good about myself as a person. I reject this false belief. I refuse to base my self-worth on my performance. I will not live by this lie any longer.* (Note how forcefully Bill rejected his false belief.)

You selected a painful situation in your life, and using the principles of The Trip In, you discovered the emotion and found the controlling false belief. Now write a forceful rejection of that false belief. To practice this process, say your forceful rejection out loud before writing it below.

_____

_____

You can learn to detect your false beliefs and reject them.

When we first begin to recognize our false beliefs, we gloss over them and rush to affirm our worth. The false beliefs remain in our mind, unchallenged and unchanged. They keep their unconscious influence and cause more destructive reactions in the future. You can learn to detect your false beliefs and reject them.

106

For example, some people might have told Bill he was wrong to resent his boss and coworkers. They would advise Bill to confess, pray, and change his behavior. Such advice is effective as far as it goes. If Bill confessed a wrong attitude about his boss and coworkers and aired his resentment, he might feel some immediate relief and think somewhat better about himself—at least he would accept the responsibility for his actions.

However, if this is all Bill does, likely he still will harbor the unconscious false belief that really caused his harmful emotions and behavior in the first place. Bill would change his attitude only temporarily; then he probably would fall back into the same behavior pattern again and probably would feel even more guilty for his failure. Bill needed a mind change about his specific false belief. Bill began to reject that false belief and refused to live on the basis of it.

Had Bill not done the work described here he might have been so depressed that he would have avoided other responsibilities at work. Step 3 in your Trip In, then, is to reject your false beliefs each time they affect you. Use self-talk. For example, if you are seeking to renew your mind by rejecting the false belief, say something like the following: *I reject this false belief. I am not going to base my worth on what other people think about me any longer. My day of being a people-pleaser is over, once and for all. I am through!* Try this exercise for yourself in the margin box. Practice makes perfect!

Let every disturbing situation be an opportunity to focus on a false belief that affects you. Focus on your false beliefs again and again, in various types of problem situations, until you become highly conscious of them. This lifts your false beliefs from your unconscious into your conscious awareness! This way you can confront those false beliefs directly, consistently, and forcefully.

Correcting by Affirming

Rejection alone isn't enough to rid your mind of false beliefs. To correct false beliefs, reject your false beliefs about specific situations. Reject all the false beliefs about your personal worth by saying the affirmation "My Identity in Christ," provided on page 113 in this book.

You reject your false beliefs and then correct them by affirming the truth about your worth as a person. Remind yourself of your identity in Christ so that eventually you can believe it with assurance and deep conviction.

Rejection alone isn't enough to rid your mind of false beliefs.

Repeat from memory the affirmation "My Identity in Christ." Then write below about a typical, predictable situation in your life in which you will commit to using the affirmation to reject false beliefs.

_____

_____

Celebrate each time you affirm your personal worth. You can tell yourself, *How marvelous it is to know I am a new creation of infinite worth! I really can believe this, so I don't have to feel like a person of low self-worth. I can regret this painful situation but don't have to overreact to it.* Make certain that each time you take The Trip In, you follow through and take all four steps so that every Trip In always ends in a celebration of your identity in Christ.

People often have a mental block against taking this kind of inner look because deep inside they fear what they see will make them feel even worse about themselves. You can keep that from happening if during The Trip In you reject your false self-concept and celebrate your worth as a person!

You will find that the task of reversing years of false beliefs about yourself and affirming a different self-concept is a long process. Here are several things to keep in mind about how to affirm your worth:

1. Merely affirming your identity in Christ does not mean your mind instantly agrees with what you are affirming. Affirming is a way by which you get a truth into your belief or value system. Repeat your affirmation insistently, over and over, until you can accept the affirmation as truth deep inside you.
2. Remember that you are affirming a new truth. You can satisfy your mind about believing you are a loved and forgiven child of God. Be convinced of the truth you are affirming.
3. Affirm the truth of your identity in Christ about specific false beliefs as they relate to a particular life situation.
4. Take the time to think through the affirmation about your worth as a loved and forgiven child of God until you really sense the full meaning of your affirmation. Consciously realizing the logic in the truth it contains, not mechanically uttering this affirmation, can correct your false beliefs.

In the steps you just read, go back and underline the portion you feel represents the biggest challenge for you. Stop and pray, asking God to help you with that challenge.

Day 5
Step 4: How Will I Act?

So far this week we have learned to: (1) determine the source of destructive thoughts or behavior; (2) discover the harmful emotions; (3) detect and reject the false belief(s); and (4) take action befitting the loved and forgiven child of God that you really are.

To correct false beliefs about ourselves, we affirm the truth about our identity in Christ. You can know you have affirmed a truth into your belief system when you begin to act in line with what you believe. You can act and think like the loved and forgiven child of God you see yourself to be. Read the verse in the margin (James 1:23-24) about hearing and doing godly actions.

> If anyone is a hearer of the word and not a doer, he is like a man who looks at his natural face in a mirror, for once he has looked at himself and gone away, he has immediately forgotten what kind of person he was.
> James 1:23-24

Today we are learning the fourth step in The Trip In. Think how you would act in a certain situation if you really believed your identity in Christ. Take that action! Your action in response to distressing situations can reinforce your faith in the person of worth you are! The moment you act is the moment when life change occurs.

In our earlier example, if Bill truly believed in his identity in Christ and acted in a way befitting the person of worth he believed himself to be, he might continue to feel the hurt but would forgive his boss for his wounding words. Hopefully Bill's boss would understand about Bill's being late, but if not, Bill still could choose to focus on his identity in Christ. He would act out that belief by making good choices in his relationships and in his work that day.

Think about the painful situation you described in day 2. Now describe how you would act in that situation if you truly believed you were a loved and forgiven child of God.

_____

_____

The Holy Spirit Helps

New actions never come easy. At times it may seem as though you have no assistance. But later you can look back on the situation and realize the Holy Spirit worked on your behalf as you took your positive and willful action. He enables you to do things you can't begin to explain in human terms!

Recall John's story in the opening case study (p. 98). Acting in line with the loved and forgiven child of God you are will lead you to admit mistakes, make amends, and correct errors whenever possible. It might release you to set goals. To act in light of your self-worth may free you to disclose thoughts and feelings without worry about pleasing others. You may attempt tasks that fear of failure kept you from trying.

Truths I Have Discovered About Myself

_____

_____

_____

_____

In the margin write the truths about yourself you have discovered as you rejected your false beliefs in day 4. Ask the Father to help you act in a way befitting a loved and forgiven child of God.

What you do in such situations indeed is your choice. You can choose to let your feelings control you, or you can choose to act in light of your identity in Christ! As you begin to act on your identity in Christ in various situations, your action reinforces your belief. You can establish a positive cycle, and you can change your entire life-style. You eventually can find it easier to believe yourself to be the person of worth that you really are.

The Next Step

Hopefully, you have learned in *The Search for Significance Workbook* how to use your emotions to identify your beliefs, so you can reject Satan's lies and replace them with God's truths. But do not expect perfection! You have built your existing belief system over a period of many years. Sometimes replacing lies with the truth may seem easy, while at other times it may be frustrating.

The enemy of our souls does not want us to be freed from his lies. Expect spiritual battles, uneasy feelings, and some discouragement. The enemy wants to confuse you and to muddle your thinking. Be patient and persistent. As you apply these principles, the time interval between your painful emotions and your ability to replace lies with God's truths can become shorter and shorter.

Then teach these truths to others. Teaching is the best way to learn because we pay more attention and study more diligently when we communicate scriptural truths to someone else.

Develop a godly tenacity and keep following Christ. You may make mistakes; you may encounter others' disapproval; you may blame someone; you may fail to apply these truths; and you occasionally may dishonor the Lord. But realize that you are deeply loved, completely forgiven, fully pleasing, totally accepted, and absolutely complete because Christ died for you and was raised from the dead to give you new life! You are free to "proclaim the excellencies of Him who has called you out of darkness into His marvelous light" (1 Peter 2:9). The Lord is for you! He gives you wisdom, strength, and encouragement—so keep at it!

Where Do You Go from Here?
Congratulations! You likely experienced change and growth as you completed your work in *The Search for Significance*. Now you may wonder what additional opportunities for growth exist.

Think about areas in your life in which you need to grow. On the following list check your top three priorities.

____ Understanding the Bible
____ Memorizing Scripture
____ Developing your prayer life
____ Building witnessing skills
____ Changing unhealthy relationships
____ Knowing God's will
____ Becoming a disciple maker
____ Caring for your physical needs
____ Other: _____

Remember that character development and spiritual growth are not instantaneous. Worthwhile goals take time.

Apply what you've learned by—
• understanding the false beliefs;
• rejecting lies and replacing them with God's truths;
• preparing yourself for spiritual battles;
• being patient and persistent;
• teaching these truths to others;
• continuing to follow Christ.

The Lord is for you! He gives you wisdom, strength, and encouragement—so keep at it.

Remember that character development and spiritual growth are not instantaneous. Worthwhile goals take time.

The Trip In

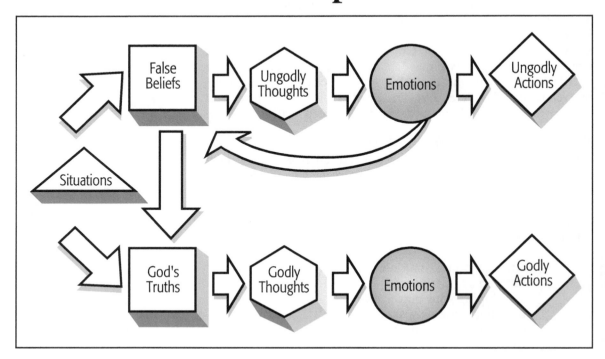

When a situation arises, we make a choice as to whether we are going to respond with a false belief or God's truth. If we choose a false belief, we begin a journey that will take us through ungodly thoughts and emotions to ungodly actions. However, the diagram above shows the process to get back on track. We can examine the emotions that result from a false belief. Then we can reject the false belief and replace it with God's truth. The truth will lead us through godly thoughts and emotions to godly actions.

These are the basic steps to be taken for a successful Trip In.
- Select as a starting point an unpleasant situation that has happened to you within the past week. Identify the destructive words/behaviors that accompanied it.
- Look inside yourself to sift through various feelings until you discover the underlying painful emotion triggering your outward behavior.
- Move through your emotions to detect the false beliefs causing your painful emotion.
- After you detect the false beliefs and reject them, affirm the truth about your special worth as a person. Go above and beyond the situation by taking action in line with the loved and forgiven child of God you see yourself to be!

My Identity in Christ

Because of Christ's redemption
I am a new creation of great worth.

I am deeply loved,
completely forgiven,
fully pleasing,
totally accepted by God,
and absolutely complete in Christ.

There has never been another person like me
in the history of humankind,
nor will there ever be.
God has made me an original,
one of a kind, really somebody!

Leading a Study of *The Search for Significance Workbook*

Before you begin your group, read and complete each step described for an organized and effective study of *The Search for Significance Workbook*. The steps will provide you with important information such as how to start a group; leader qualifications and skills, promotional efforts, and ordering information.

Steps for Starting a Group

The following steps can help you prepare to minister effectively through group study. Check each of the steps as you complete this overview.

- ❏ Prayer
- ❏ Facilitator Qualifications
- ❏ Skills for Leading a *Search* Group
- ❏ Foundational Concepts
- ❏ Enlisting a Coleader
- ❏ Setting a Time, Date, and Place
- ❏ Ordering Materials
- ❏ Promotional Efforts
- ❏ Setting Fees
- ❏ Deciding on Child Care
- ❏ Getting Started

Step 1
Prayer

Prayer is the essential ingredient for any church ministry. God has a vital interest in persons who seek after Him. This includes those in the church and those outside the church.

Begin praying by asking God to bring to this group those persons He has selected. As group leader you will want to pray for each group member during the week. You likely will pray for them at other times, such as during the group process.

Begin your preparation time with prayer, and bathe everything you do in prayer because prayer unleashes the power of God to work in the lives of people.

Step 2
Facilitator Qualifications

Ideally, the leader will be a facilitator rather than a teacher. The facilitator guides the group process and allows the group members to share information and process their own feelings about certain issues that rise out of the discussions.

The requirements necessary for a person to lead a group are to—
- be a growing Christian with a personal relationship with Jesus Christ;
- be a person of prayer,
- be an active member of a church;
- have a sense of God's call to this group;
- be spiritually gifted for the work;
- have a knowledge of Scripture;
- have a commitment to keep confidential information private;
- be willing to give time and energy to help members of the group;
- have a teachable spirit;
- be sensitive to the leadership of the Holy Spirit in a person's life;
- love the Lord and people.

If you are enlisting the facilitator, pray over these leader qualifications. Ask God to make clear His choice for a leader. If you are the facilitator, you may feel less than adequate in some areas, but if God has invited you to join Him in this ministry, He will gift you for this task.

God is looking for caring people who can empathize with group members at the point of their greatest needs. Let God be your guide and your enabler in this endeavor. Allow Him to work through you and to touch lives through your life.

Step 3
Skills for Leading a *Search* Group

We now will examine in detail the skills that describe a good group leader.

Be a good communicator.
Communication involves both verbal and nonverbal skills. The shape of your mouth, the look in your eyes, and the intensity of your brow communicate to the group members what you really are feeling. Communicate with group members, listen to what they say, but be certain to observe their nonverbal communication as well.

Be a good listener.
Listening is a skill that everyone can develop to a greater degree. Give your undivided attention when a group member shares. Keep your eyes on the person and listen to him or her alone. Avoid thinking about what you plan to say next. From time to time give the person verbal feedback, such as "I agree," "I understand," "I know what you are saying," or "Yes." Listening is a skill that a person develops by practicing it in real life situations.

Be a servant leader.
A group leader models that he or she is also a traveler on the journey of spiritual growth. Only by modeling your own spiritual journey of trials and hardships, mountaintops and valleys will you model this behavior to the group.

Be an encourager.
Set the example by encouraging the group members continually. Each week promote the idea that members will find ways to encourage a person in the group. Without the skill of encouragement your group session will be nothing more than a time of processing information. Your encouragement will make a difference when members feel discouraged or when they feel like dropping out of the group.

Know how to keep one person from dominating.
The leader keeps the group on target. A group member who dominates the group discussion can damage the dynamics of the group process and can keep the group from participating in the assigned tasks. Very subtly interrupt the dominating person. Ask for a more direct answer to your question or ask him or her to let the other group members respond.

Know how to refer persons for professional help.
You may discover that a particular member of the group needs professional Christian help. Avoid allowing group members to deny emotional and behavioral problems by coloring them in religious phrases. If this type of situation arises, do not hesitate to recommend the need for professional help. Ask your pastor or appropriate staff member for their help.

Know how to involve members in discussion.
The lecture method is not suitable in a group. If this is the only method with which you feel comfortable, do not attempt to lead a group. Each session contains interaction between all of the group members. Make it possible for every group member to participate in the group process.

Know how to be personally involved without relinquishing leadership.
From the beginning help the group recognize that you are a fellow struggler. Never dominate the group, but take time to share your own faults, frailties, and fears as they pertain to the discussion. Let group members see you as one of them, but as the leader of the group, always be in control of the group process so that every aspect of the week's work can be covered in the appropriate time frame. Be yourself, be real, be honest, but always remember that your primary responsibility as the group leader is to lead group members in their search for significance.

Be ready for anything.
Be sensitive to what the Holy Spirit wants to accomplish. As you allow Him to guide you and the group, God will use the discussions to accomplish His purposes. Do not be so rigid and fixed on your agenda that you cannot focus on what God is doing in the group.

Step 4
Foundational Concepts

Members will be asked to attend the group sessions.
One of the essential elements in the group process is participation by every group member.. None of these elements will develop properly if the group members do not attend the group sessions. Otherwise, the sense of trust and bonding in fellowship among members never will materialize.

Members will maintain confidentiality.
Trust among the group members is an essential element of the group process. Stress confidentiality in group discussions. Inform members that they must not tell anyone's story except their own.

Members will be open to a Christ-centered approach to this study in a small-group setting.
Unchurched individuals well may become a part of the group process. These individuals should be open to a Christ-centered approach and understand that group members will be encouraged to keep Christ at the center of all they say and do.

Step 5
Enlisting a Coleader

Pray about finding someone who will go through the study as a participant but who also displays a desire or the skills to lead a group later. You may want to choose from among individuals who sign up for the group but let them know your agenda early on.

Step 6
Setting a Time, Date, and Place

A *Search* group can meet at a time most convenient for the members. That time might be when other church activities are occurring. Arrange for the group to meet in the same place each week, preferably at the church. Use movable furniture. The lesson plan is set up for one to one and a half hours. Adjust group activities if you go over this time.

Step 7
Ordering Materials

Order sufficient copies of the study well in advance of your first session. Ask for *The Search for Significance Workbook* (item 001244374), one copy for each group member.

You can purchase materials at your local LifeWay Christian Store or order them from LifeWay Resources Customer Service (see p. 2 for additional ordering information).

Step 8
Promotional Efforts

Before you start, schedule at least a four-week period for registration and promotion of the group. Determine your target audience. If you plan to target only church members, then use the normal channels of promotion in your church, such as the church newsletter, the church website, posters, or bulletin inserts. Hopefully, your pastor would give his endorsement.

If you plan to offer the study to the unchurched—an approach that is highly needed—then place an advertisement in the local newspaper, on Christian radio, or on flyers placed in businesses. This study can become a tremendous outreach vehicle for the church. Many people today are looking for answers and the encouragement and support a group can give them. They also need Scriptural support for the truth that comes from God and not the world.

Step 9
Setting Fees

Ask group members to pay for their own Bible study books. You may consider an additional charge beyond the materials' cost to provide scholarships for persons who cannot afford to buy their own books, or to purchase supplies needed for carrying out the leader plan. Asking the members of the group to pay for their books helps communicate the level of commitment you expect from them.

Charging for the books also allows the person to feel as if he or she is contributing something to the ministry. This especially helps unchurched persons who also might want to join the group. To protect your church from legal liability, do not charge fees for the group session or pay the facilitator of the group. This is a lay-led group, not a professionally led group.

Step 10
Deciding on Child Care

Decide whether you will want to provide child care for the children of group members. Child care will allow some people who otherwise could not participate to join the group. The best solution is for the group members to arrange child care on their own. If possible, meet during regular church activities when child care is provided.

Step 11
Getting Started

Familiarize yourself with the first three weeks of the Bible study book and the leader guide. This step will help you become familiar with the homework and the basic outline for the group sessions. Complete the first week in the Bible study book and review the leader guide before you start group session 1.

In planning activities for your weekly group sessions, you likely will find that far more activities are provided than you will have time to accomplish during the period allotted. Select the activities that you feel are the most relevant to your group's learning experience.

Your Role as a Facilitator

1. Model the role by completing the assignments, including the learning activities.
2. Keep the group moving through the material. Avoid telling your own stories at the expense of the group's participation.

Introduction Session (Optional)

Before the Session

1. Read and be prepared to overview the introduction (pp. 4–7).
2. Read "During the Session." Select the activities that will best suit prospective attendees. Adapt or develop other activities that you sense will best help your group benefit from the week of study.
3. Collect needed supplies, such as Bible study books, Bibles, markers, name tags, pencils or pens, and a basket for collecting money. Place supplies on a table near the door.
4. Prepare an attendance sheet with room for a name, daytime phone number or email address for each member. Place this sheet on the table, as well.
5. Arrange the chairs in a semicircle facing a marker board or wall space you will use to mount posters or tear sheets (focal wall). Sit as a member of the group.
6. Monitor your usage of time. Always begin and close on time. Your group will learn to abide by these boundaries if you do.

During the Session

1. As participants arrive, ask them to sign in and complete the name tags (optional). Give them a copy of the Bible study book. Invite them to leave payment for the book in the basket now or at the end of the session.
2. Welcome the group. Introduce yourself and ask the others to do the same. Begin with prayer.
3. Give members an overview of the Introduction. Have them follow along as you talk through pages 4–7. Then point them to the affirmation, "My Identity in Christ," on page 113. Say the Identity statement together. Have volunteers read the course map showing the false beliefs and God's truth (p. 128).
4. Encourage participants to share what they have seen and read that excites them about this study. Write responses on a marker board or another surface.
5. Assign week 1 in the Bible study book for discussion at the next group session. Suggest that they follow the plan of reading each day's material, rather than saving it all for one or two study sessions. Encourage them to complete each learning activity for greater retention of the material.
6. Urge members not only to attend but also to be prompt to avoid unnecessary interruptions.
7. Close by asking God to give each of you open hearts to learn and grow as they commit to this study.

After Each Session

1. Use the attendance sheet to identify anyone who missed the session. Contact absentees during the week between each session.
2. Remember to pray for each person. As the weeks go by, you will learn specific things to pray for on their behalf.

Session 1
The Search Begins

Before the Session

1. If you chose not to have an introduction session, include the overview of the Introduction (pp. 4–7) in session 1.
2. Read "During the Session."
3. Decide on the amount of time that you want to allow for each activity. Always be prepared to change your plans as the Holy Spirit leads and as needs of the group dictate.
4. Have on hand a marker board and markers, or plan to display a poster or tear sheets on a focal wall.
5. Arrange the chairs in a semicircle facing the focal wall in each session.
6. Make a T-chart by drawing a line down the middle of a poster. Bring two additional posters or tear sheets for group discussion.

7. Prepare a two-minute preview of week 2.
8. Decide how you will use the plan of salvation (p. 22) during the session.

During the Session

1. Greet members as they arrive.
2. Get acquainted. If members do not know one another well, ask them to share information about themselves.
3. Thank God for bringing this group together. Ask the Holy Spirit to be your Teacher.

Group Sharing Time

1. Together find Romans 12:2 in your Bibles and read the verse aloud. Ask the group to brainstorm ways their thinking is conformed to the pattern of this world. On the T chart, write these ideas in the left column.
2. Now ask the group to brainstorm ways their thinking can be transformed by the renewing of their minds. Write these in the right column. Say: "*The Search for Significance Workbook* will help you to reject the thinking pattern of this world and to accept the truth set forth in God's Word."
3. Ask volunteers to share ways that God has personally taught them a new truth.
4. Ask each person to share one way he or she strives for self-worth or personal significance. As group members volunteer their answers, write each answer on the markerboard or poster board.
5. After all have shared, ask members to determine which ways are performance-based, and place a P by these; place an A for approval based; and then ask them to identify a G by the ways which are based on God's truth. Tell the group that too often people base their personal significance on how well they perform as persons and on the opinions of others.
6. Recall the story of Dave from page 8. Ask: "Which letter would you place by his name: P, A, or G?"

7. Ask several to tell their definitions of self-worth. Arrive at a group consensus of the definition. Write this definition on the marker board or poster board. Compare the statement with the one written on page 12.
8. Ask them to share their understanding of the key words for week 1: *redemption* and *unconditional*. Review page 22.
9. Ask several to share from week 1 a statement that had an impact on their understanding of who they are and why they are here. Also ask members to share other insights from this week's lessons.

Small-Group Sharing Time

1. Be prepared to divide your group into triads during small-group sharing time. Join a group of two if you are needed to make a threesome; otherwise, pray silently alone.
2. Tell group members that each week they will break up in triads to pray together and to review memorization assignments. These triads will represent their permanent small groups for the next 5 weeks. Each member will be invited to contact his or her triad regularly to offer encouragement and affirmation to continue this search.
3. Do not appoint members to a group. Let them self-select. However, discourage spouses to be in the same group. Ask triads to pull their chairs together.
4. Ask each small group to work on memorizing the key verse for week 1. Ask members to repeat the verse to one another once they feel comfortable doing so.
5. If time permits, ask them to begin memorizing the first false belief found on page 128.
6. When three to five minutes are left in the small-group time, ask groups to move into their prayer time. Be sensitive to the fact that some may be uncomfortable praying aloud.

Closure

1. Bring the groups back together.

2. Give your two-minute review of week 2 and make the assignment to complete it.
3. Stand and join hands. Ask those who feel comfortable doing so to say aloud a one-sentence prayer in which each person personally commits himself or herself to God for the duration of this course.

After the Session
1. Use your attendance sheet to pray for each person this week. Identify any group member that you already know has special needs. Consult your pastor if you feel these needs are too great for you to manage.
2. Call all members of your group to encourage them and to remind them of their commitment to the other group members.
3. If a member of the group does not evidence a personal salvation experience, make certain that you share the plan of salvation with that person privately.
4. Prepare for your next group session.

Session 2
Satan's Lies

Before the Session
1. Read "During the Session."
2. Use a marker board, or display a poster board on the focal wall.
3. Prepare a two-minute preview of unit 3.

During the Session
1. Greet members as they arrive.
2. Ask each person to silently pray a one-sentence prayer for personal needs that can be touched by this study. Close the prayer time with your own prayer.

Group Sharing Time
1. Ask everyone to turn to the course map on page 128. Tell the group that the discussion in this session will center around the false beliefs: I must meet certain standards

to feel good about myself and I must have the approval of certain others to feel good about myself.
2. Brainstorm characteristics of God. Write these on poster board. Compare this description with how they would describe God if they believed the first of Satan's lies—the performance trap. Then ask members to describe God from the viewpoint of an approval addict.
3. Ask the group to share ways they react to the first and second of Satan's deceptions. Ask volunteers to share a personal experience that illustrates their deception.
4. Ask members to turn to page 24. Enlist several to share the standards they recorded and point out which of the standards are performance-based.
5. Review three ways we react to Satan's deception (pp. 25–26). Ask volunteers to give examples of how fear of failure affects our lives (pp. 28–30).
6. Ask others to give examples of how fear of rejection affects our lives (pp. 32–37).
7. Ask everyone to turn to page 37. In unison read 1 Corinthians 10:31. Say that self-worth is secure in Christ. Encourage them to remember that gaining God's acceptance is not proper motivation for what they do, because those in Jesus Christ are totally accepted by God. We obey to give God glory.
8. If time permits, let group members share other insights from this week's lessons.

Small-Group Sharing Time
1. Ask group members to join together in their triads to work together on memorizing the key verse for week 2 and the first and second false beliefs.
2. When three to five minutes are left in the small-group time, ask members to pray for one another's needs.

Closure
1. Bring the groups back together. Remind

triads to regularly encourage one another with a call, email, or personal note.
2. Give your two-minute review of week 3 and make the assignment to complete it.
3. Stand and join hands. Ask volunteers to pray aloud a one-sentence prayer for God to work in lives of group members in the coming weeks.

After the Session

1. Keep your list of participants with you and pray for each one this week. Pray specifically for any member with special needs.
2. Take a few moments to evaluate how each member of the group participates in the sharing time. Ask God to give you wisdom to involve all the members of the group during sharing and discussion times.
3. Make a special point to call absentees to encourage him or her to attend the next group meeting.
4. Prepare for your next group session.

Session 3
God's Truths

Before the Session

1. Read "During the Session."
2. Provide a piece of paper and pencil for each person.
3. If you do not use a marker board, bring poster board or tear sheets.
4. Prepare a two-minute preview of week 4.

During the Session

1. Greet members as they arrive. Practice saying in unison the first two of Satan's Lies.
2. Ask each person to pray silently a one-sentence prayer for personal needs that can be touched by this study. Then close in prayer.

Group Sharing Time

1. Ask everyone to turn to the course map on page 128.

2. Tell the group that the discussion in this session will center around the first of God's truth statements (p. 128).

Because of justification I am completely forgiven by and fully pleasing to God. I no longer have to fear failure.

3. Ask a volunteer to read Romans 5:1, the key verse for week 3. Share with the group that their justification is through Christ's death, not their perfection. Review the definition of *justify* from page 38.
4. Distribute paper and pencils. Invite members to draw a T-chart ledger sheet and label the right column My Sins and the left Christ's Righteousness. In privacy, tell them to (1) list 5 sins they have committed, and (2) assign a number from 1 to 10 for each sin. Add the total. Then put the same total in the right column. Point out that Christ has taken all our sin on Him. What we "owe" is zero, based on Christ's Righteousness.
5. Ask: "What should be our motivation for obedience to the commands of God [pp. 42–49]? What would be poor motivations for obedience [pp. 50–52]?"
6. Ask a volunteer to state the differences between punishment and discipline. Then ask: "How can we know which is which?" Write responses on the marker board/poster.
7. Ask a volunteer to read "Changing the Way You Do Things" on page 52.
8. If time permits, let group members share other insights from this week's lessons.

Small-Group Sharing Time

1. In triads, ask small-group members to work together on memorizing the key verse for week 3 and the first statement of God's Truth (p. 128).
2. When three to five minutes are left in the small-group time, ask members to pray for one another's needs.

Closure

1. Bring the groups back together. Ask individuals who have memorized the first lie and the first truth (p. 128) to say them in unison.
2. Give your two-minute review of week 4 and make the assignment to complete it.
3. Ask a volunteer to pray aloud that God's Spirit would continue to work in the lives of each person in the group.

After the Session

1. Use your attendance sheet to pray for each one specifically this week.
2. Call members of your group this week to encourage them, especially if they seem to have difficulty finishing the homework.
3. Evaluate the group dynamics of this session. Who is doing most of the sharing? volunteering? Who is not participating? Ask for God's wisdom as you seek His leadership.
4. Prepare for your next group session.

Session 4
The Performance Trap

Before the Session

1. Read "During the Session."
2. Provide paper and pencils.
3. If you do not use a marker board, bring poster board or tear sheets.
4. Prepare a two-minute preview of week 5.

During the Session

1. Greet members as they arrive.
2. Begin with reading the key verse for week 4. Pray, asking God to show us His wisdom in our most private and most vulnerable areas.

Group Sharing Time

1. Ask everyone to turn to the course map on page 128. Tell them this session will probe more deeply into a performance-based mentality.

2. Review Don's experience (p. 53). Lead the group to relate similar experiences in their lives or the lives of others.
3. Select three people to read the questions at the top of page 54. Discuss questions 1 and 3.
4. Compare the lure of success with a plastic worm on a fishing rod. Success can't give a real sense of self-worth. It's an imitation.
5. Distribute paper and pencils. Ask each person privately to write a brief description of the ways they are most likely to feel the performance trap. Don't ask anyone to share their answers, but they may volunteer if they wish. Then discuss in general terms ways to combat Satan's trap (pp. 57–59).
6. Discuss why we grow impatient with our spiritual growth. List ways to enhance it.
7. Write the equation on page 67 on the marker board or poster board. Then, make the equal sign an unequal sign by placing a vertical line through it. Rewrite the equation with the right answer to give us self-worth. (Example: Self-worth equals God's love and forgiveness permeating all areas of our lives.)
8. If time permits let group members share other insights from this week's lessons.

Small-Group Sharing Time

1. Ask members to join together in their triads. Make the following assignment. As a group, write a possible ending to the story of Jane (p. 55) to reflect her healing from the performance trap.
2. Ask members of the small groups to work together on memorizing the key verse for week 4 and the first seven lines of "My Identity in Christ" (p. 113).
3. When three to five minutes remain in the group time, ask them to pray individually for victory from the performance trap.

Closure

1. Bring the groups back together. Ask a representative of each small group to share their endings to Jane's story.

2. Give your two-minute review of week 5 and make the assignment to complete it.
3. Stand and join hands. Ask a volunteer to pray for progress to move beyond the performance traps of member's lives.

After the Session
1. Use your attendance sheet to pray for each one specifically this week.
2. Contact absentees.
3. Prepare for your next group session.

Session 5
The Approval Addict

Before the Session
1. Read "During the Session."
2. If you do not use a marker board, bring poster board or tear sheets.
3. Prepare a two-minute preview of week 6.

During the Session
1. Welcome the group. Begin with reading the key verse for week 5.
2. Pray, asking God to show us His wisdom in our most private and most vulnerable areas.

Group Sharing Time
1. Ask everyone to turn to the course map on page 128. Tell them this session will probe more deeply into the approval addict's mentality. and God's solution for it.
2. Review the description of the approval addict from the bottom of page 68. Discuss the meaning of reconciliation and mercy.
3. Ask members to share about the person whose approval they need most and whose rejection they fear most. Ask them to use very general terms such as *coworker, relative,* or *teacher,* not specific terms such as the names of individuals.
4. Share an insight about your need for approval and ask other group members to share also. Point out that wanting people's

approval is not wrong in itself but tying self-worth to others' approval is a false belief and can make a person an approval addict.
5. Ask the members to share how much they are affected by the second false belief. Then say that only when people realize the impact of this false belief on their lives can they begin the process of allowing God to set them free from Satan's lie.
6. Ask the group how they have used rejection to manipulate other people. Strive to help the group arrive at a clear understanding of how rejection makes them and others feel.
7. Ask: "What does a person have to do to be accepted by you?" After discussion ends, enlist a volunteer to read the four levels of rejection on page 74.
8. Ask members to share how they can communicate unconditional acceptance to children without approving of their unacceptable behavior.
9. Write the equation on page 67 on the marker board or poster board. Then, make the equal sign an unequal sign by placing a vertical line through it. Rewrite the equation with the right answer to give us self-worth. (Example: Self-worth equals God's love and forgiveness permeating all areas of our life.)
10. Have members turn to page 75. Select individuals to read what they wrote for the first activity. Point out that the Scriptures demonstrate the theme of reconciliation in the Bible.
11. If time permits let group members share other insights from this week's lessons.

Small-Group Sharing Time
1. In triads give each group one of the following assignments: Tell us how the following characters can break the cycle of approval addiction: Helen (p. 68), Edith (pp. 71–72, 82) or Janet (p. 76–77).

2. Then ask groups to work together on memorizing the week 5 key verse and seven lines of "My Identity in Christ" (p. 113).
3. When three to five minutes remain in group time, ask them to pray for victory from approval addiction.

Closure

1. Bring the groups back together. Allow volunteers to give the group reports on the three women.
2. Give your two-minute review of week 5 and make the assignment to complete it.
3. Stand and join hands. Ask a volunteer to pray for our intention to seek God's approval rather than others.

After the Session

1. Use your attendance sheet to pray for each person specifically this week.
2. Contact absentees.
3. Prepare for your next group session.

Session 6
Guilt and Conviction

Before the Session

1. Read "During the Session."
2. If you do not use a marker board, bring poster board or tear sheets.
3. Prepare a two-minute preview of week 7.

During the Session

1. Welcome the group. Begin with reading the key verse for week 6.
2. Pray, asking God to show us how to live courageously, without fear of shame.

Group Sharing Time

1. Ask everyone to turn to the course map on page 128. Tell them this session will cover the third and fourth of Satan's lies and God's truth. Select volunteers to read these aloud.

2. Ask which is the correct answer to this question: "Appropriate feelings for a Christian are (1) guilt and conviction or (2) guilt and condemnation?" Follow up by asking why they chose their response. Discuss the meaning of condemnation and why it is so destructive to a Christian.
3. Ask someone to read this week's key verse, Romans 8:1 aloud (p. 84). Ask: "If God does not condemn His children, where does the condemnation originate?"
4. Brainstorm reasons we try to blame others and distance ourselves from blame. List these on one side of the marker board.
5. Review the answers to the first activity on page 86. Discuss the role of propitiation in sparing us from condemnation. (Christ took our guilt. Only when people realize the impact of guilt on their lives can they begin to allow God to set them free from Satan's lie.)
6. Ask a volunteer to explain the difference between blame and shame. Then brainstorm the negative effects of shame. Write these on the other side of the marker board.
7. Ask: "What is God's answer to shame?" Discuss the meaning of *regeneration* (p. 92). Invite testimonies about changes members have made as a result of the new birth.
8. Review the contrasting purposes and results of guilt and conviction (pp. 93–94).
9. Read the definition of forgiveness on page 96 and lead the group to respond to each of the activities.
10. If time permits, let group members share other insights from this week's lessons.

Small-Group Sharing Time

1. In triads, give each group one of the following assignments: As a group, write how the following characters can break the cycle of shame and blame: Matt (pp. 86–87), Tom (p. 88) or Jeff (pp. 90–91).
2. Then ask the small groups to work together on memorizing the third and fourth lie and God's truth.

3. When three to five minutes remain in group time, ask them to pray for victory from feelings of blame and shame.

Closure

1. Bring the groups back together. Allow volunteers to give the group reports on the three men.
2. Give your two-minute review of week 7 and make the assignment to complete it.
3. Stand and join hands. Ask a volunteer to pray for newness in the lives of believers who have asked God for changes.

After the Session

1. Use your attendance sheet to pray for each person specifically this week.
2. Make an effort to have every member present for the final session.
3. Prepare for your last group session.

Session 7
The Trip In

Before the Session

1. Read "During the Session."
2. On poster board, write the five actions of a Trip In from the margin of page 101.
3. If you choose to make truth cards, bring needed materials (p. 100).
4. Note that there is no small-group time.

During the Session

1. Welcome the group. Thank members for their participation during the study. Be sensitive to the Holy Spirit, allowing testimonies about ways God has worked during the past seven weeks. Close with prayer.
2. Draw the group's attention to the poster you prepared. Keep it before the group as you discuss the four steps in the Trip In.
3. Ask a volunteer to share from page 102 how people process their emotions until they arrive at the one affecting their behavior.

4. Ask why repressing feelings derails The Trip In. Then call on someone to read the three main benefits in identifying the underlying emotion (p. 103).
5. Ask someone to share why he or she believes it is necessary to link the emotion with a particular false belief.
6. Review The Why Formula on page 104. If someone has had an experience similar to that of Bill, suggest that he or she tell the story. Then, as a group, determine the painful emotions and false beliefs.
7. Ask volunteers to select one of the four false beliefs and model to the rest of the group self-talk for that false belief. Allow time for constructive comments concerning the forcefulness and believability of the member's self-talk.
8. Point out that rejecting false beliefs isn't enough to correct them. Make it a habit to say from memory the four false beliefs, the four truths, and the positive affirmation of "My Identity in Christ." Then lead them to say from memory these statements.
9. Select four members to read the four statements at the end of page 108.
10. Brainstorm practical ways you can begin to act in line with the loved and accepted child of God that you are in God's sight. (see p. 111).
11. Take the rest of the time to allow members to share insights they have come to understand, things God has already begun to do in their lives, and how they see God using *The Search for Significance Workbook* in the days ahead.

Closure

Ask members to stand and join hands. Ask each person to affirm the work of God in the person on his or her left. Then affirm the person on his or her right. Close with a prayer rejoicing for each step forward that has been taken in the freedom that God has brought to each person's life.

Meet the Author

Robert S. McGee

Dr. McGee is a professional counselor and lecturer. He is currently the president of Search Ministries.

Dr. McGee is founder of Rapha, a nationally recognized health-care organization that provides in-hospital and outpatient care with a Christ-centered perspective for adults and adolescents suffering with psychiatric and substance-abuse problems.

More than two million people from almost one hundred countries around the world have read *The Search for Significance*. It has been used to touch people who have learned for the first time that God truly does love them and can free them from the unrealistic standards and expectations of others.

Continue the Search...

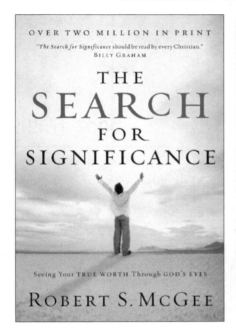

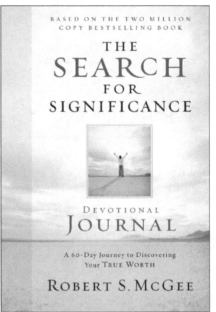

Also available in audio cassette and CD

Available from

W PUBLISHING GROUP
A Division of Thomas Nelson Publishers
Since 1798

For other life-changing resources, visit us at:
www.thomasnelson.com

	False Beliefs	**God's Truths**

The Performance Trap

I must meet certain standards to feel good about myself. (Fear of failure)

Because of *justification* I am completely forgiven by and fully pleasing to God. I no longer have to fear failure.

Approval Addict

I must have the approval of certain others to feel good about myself. (Fear of rejection)

Because of *reconciliation* I am totally accepted by God. I no longer have to fear rejection.

The Blame Game

Those who fail (including myself) are unworthy of love and deserve to be punished. (Guilt)

Because of *propitiation* I am deeply loved by God. I no longer have to fear punishment or punish others.

Shame

I am what I am. I cannot change. I am hopeless. (Shame)

Because of *regeneration* I have been made brand-new, complete in Christ. I no longer need to experience the pain of shame.